Zing!

Seven
Creativity
Practices
for
Educators
and
Students

To the authors whose books have taught and delighted me through the years and to the bold, creative educators who inspire me by their commitment to the underserved

Zing!

Seven
Creativity
Practices
for
Educators
and
Students

PAT MORA

CORWIN
A SAGE Company

For information:

Corwin
A SAGE Company
2455 Teller Road
Thousand Oaks, California 91320
(800) 233-9936
Fax: (800) 417-2466
www.corwin.com

SAGE Ltd.
1 Oliver's Yard
55 City Road
London EC1Y 1SP
United Kingdom

SAGE India Pvt. Ltd.
B 1/I 1 Mohan Cooperative
Industrial Area
Mathura Road,
New Delhi 110 044
India

SAGE Asia-Pacific Pte. Ltd.
33 Pekin Street #02-01
Far East Square
Singapore 048763

Printed in the United States of America

Library of Congress Cataloging-in-Publication Data

Mora, Pat.
Zing! : seven creativity practices for educators and students / Pat Mora.
    p. cm.
Includes bibliographical references.
ISBN 978-1-4129-7839-2 (pbk.)
    1. Creative teaching. 2. Creative ability. 3. Motivation in education. I. Title.

LB1025.3.M663 2010
371.102—dc22   2009053744

This book is printed on acid-free paper.

10   11   12   13   14   10   9   8   7   6   5   4   3   2   1

Acquisitions Editor:	Dan Alpert
Associate Editor:	Megan Bedell
Production Editor:	Amy Schroller
Copy Editor:	Codi Bowman
Typesetter:	C&M Digitals (P) Ltd.
Proofreader:	Gail Fay
Cover Designer:	Rose Storey

Contents

Thanks

Gracias

My sincere thanks to my editor Dan Alpert; to production editor Amy Schroller and the staff at Corwin; to the manuscript reviewers; to my agent Elizabeth Harding and her colleague Anna Webman; to Deborah Chasman, who suggested such a book years ago; and to Ellen McIntyre, who believed in the concept. I also wish to express my gratitude to my friends Father Murray Bodo, Kay and Dan Moore, Elizabeth Mills, Carolyn Trela, and Joseph Rodriquez for their love and support; to the inspiring teachers and librarians I mention in these letters; and to all educators who have taught and teach me through their dedicated example. A special thanks to Patricia Armendariz and to Sylvia Vardell for their faith, friendship, and quick willingness to make suggestions on the manuscript and to Linda Weston for her steady, cheerful assistance. I also am indebted to three past fellowships: a National Endowment for the Arts Poetry Fellowship, a Kellogg National Leadership Fellowship, and a Civitella Ranieri Fellowship. A special thanks to the staff who administers these gifts.

Thank-you hugs to my children, Bill, Libby, and Cissy; to my supportive family, especially my sister Stella Mora Henry; and my husband, Vern Scarborough.

Finally, deep thanks to the Spirit who unites us all.

About the Author

Pat Mora, a popular presenter across the country at conferences, campuses, libraries, and schools, speaks and offers workshops on literacy, creativity, leadership, the writing process, and serving diverse populations. "Sharing Bookjoy: Creative Literacy Leaders" and "ZING! Seven Creativity Practices for Educators and Students" are among her more popular themes.

The author of award-winning books of nonfiction and poetry for adults and of many children's books, Pat received honorary doctorates in letters from North Carolina State University and SUNY Buffalo and is an honorary member of the American Library Association. Among her other awards are the 2006 National Hispanic Cultural Center Literary Award, a Civitella Ranieri Fellowship, a Visiting Carruthers Chair at the University of New Mexico, a Poetry Fellowship from the National Endowment for the Arts, and a Kellogg National Leadership Fellowship.

A former teacher, university administrator, and consultant, Pat is the founder of the family literacy initiative El día de los niños/El día de los libros, Children's Day/Book Day (known as Día), now housed at the American Library Association. The yearlong commitment to linking all children to books, languages, and cultures and of sharing what Pat calls "bookjoy" culminates in national celebrations in April.

The mother of three adult children, Pat lives in Santa Fe, New Mexico. For further information, visit www.patmora.com.

Welcome! ¡Bienvenidos!

Warm greetings! I'm writing you from my home in Santa Fe, New Mexico, and am looking out at the piñon-and-juniper-covered hills. How I wish you were here and that we were chatting face-to-face. Because good educators are creative, adept at the art of teaching, it's not surprising that some of you confide your interest in writing, painting, or photography. You ask about how I began writing. What's my process?

Your questions prompted me to think and now to write about my life and habits as a writer, speaker, educator, and advocate, to write about the zing of creating. "Zing"? I've long loved the sound and energy of this word that sings, which means zest, vitality, energy. In these letters to you, I want to share some stories and strategies and to propose seven practices I've learned that can assist us to develop our personal creativity and professional inventiveness. The letter about each practice is followed by a companion letter on nurturing the same habit in our students, suggestions for imaginative teaching.

During my school years, I grumbled about book reports, tests, and writing assignments (about memorizing prepositions and diagramming compound-complex sentences!), but early in life, I discovered *bookjoy*. Bookjoy, *la alegría en los libros,* the pure pleasure of reading, is one of my mother's many gifts to me. When I was a little girl in my hometown of El Paso, Texas, I savored poetry, biographies, *Heidi,* Nancy Drew, books by Louisa May Alcott and Laura Ingalls Wilder. How I looked forward to the time when my teachers would read a book aloud to us.

Year after year, I read, a habit that feels natural and essential as breathing. Without a book or magazine, I'll read cereal boxes, tiny words on packets of artificial sweetener. I wouldn't be me without books that have helped me savor and understand the world. Steadily,

1

books made me proud to be part of the same species as the authors, to wonder how they made their language shine.

When my three children were young, we read Mother Goose, Beatrix Potter, Little Bear, Frances, and Richard Scary books, stories by E. B. White and Maurice Sendak. All were—and are—our wild and wonderful loves. I'd occasionally muster the courage in those years to submit an essay, poem, or children's book for publication, but the rejections zipped back at a startling speed. I kept reading.

Then one day, I saw a magazine ad: white paint, on black bricks, words by the Spanish writer Cervantes, "By the street of by and by, you arrive at the house of never." I stopped, clipped the words, pasted them on my spice cabinet where I knew I'd see them when I rolled pastry for a cherry pie or grated cheese for red chile enchiladas. The age of forty was coming at me. Could I make writing a regular part of my life? The wonderful language from all the years of reading welled up; I wanted to explore sounds and notions on the page. So what practices have I learned?

An undramatic word, "practice," a sturdiness to it, faith in wise repetition.

Dancers, lawyers, scientists, musicians, inventors, physicians, and carvers—all practice. I'll use writing as my main example, but these practices assist with all kinds of creative endeavors.

Seven Creativity Practices

1. Value your creative self

2. Enjoy quiet

3. Gather your materials

4. Begin your project

5. Revise

6. Share your creations

7. Steadily persist in your creative work

In one sense, all adults are teachers. By our example, we influence others. Physicians and veterinarians educate their clients. At museums, zoos, aquariums, and community centers, staff members offer informal education. Most of the librarians and teachers I write about in these letters work in classrooms and libraries at all levels. In varying ways, the national community of educators invests its life in the next generation. I hope you know how important you are whether you work with children, teens, or adults. Teachers are powerful people in your classrooms and in society. And what a challenge you've chosen. By your example, how do you educate your students to be imaginative, literate, critical thinkers and lifelong learners? How do you guide them to be engaged, responsible, hardworking members of our democracy and our world?

Dedicated, effective teachers are wise community leaders. Treasures.

My teachers gave and give me so many gifts, my own teachers and you—the librarians and teachers who teach me now as I observe you and listen to you. This book of letters is a small thank-you.

CHAPTER ONE

Value Your Creative Self

Dear Teacher,

When my first book, *Chants,* a poetry collection for adults, was published in 1984, I began speaking and giving readings at colleges and high schools; and when my first children's book, *A Birthday Basket for Tía,* was published in 1992, I added school visits to my travels. Who wouldn't want to spend time with young readers who say with deep feeling, "You are my favorite arthur!" These visits and professional conferences not only allow me to listen to students but also to hear you talk about your current challenges and successes.

Trust your initial, spontaneous responses and jot down your answers to the following questions. Are you creative? Does the word intimidate you? Does it motivate you? What is creativity? Name some creative people and not only the famous ones. Describe their work, occupations, or professions. What interests you about creativity? I was intrigued that my son, Bill, a scientist and writer, defined it as "the ability to discover and communicate multiple, unusual solutions." He applied this to varied activities, from playing basketball to the arts. My daughter Libby, a lawyer and writer, also included the arts and aesthetic abilities but added inventive, practical, and problem-solving talent.

Thinking about the topic of innovation, I realized that I might once have answered as teachers occasionally do, "I'm not creative, but I'm organized." Some people firmly respond yea or nay often based on childhood experiences and family encouragement. People can initially equate the word "creativity" solely with the arts but then mention that creativity includes the ability to make new connections, and isn't that a major part of the teaching process? So I'm surprised when some teachers question their creativity. How can you constructively balance a room full of easily distracted bodies with different personalities, learning abilities and styles, home languages, cultures *and* teach them critical thinking and new skills? You must be creative! You may not have released all the inventiveness within you, but it's there. Women are particularly prone to doubt their talents. Those prickly doubts probably never vanish.

In a letter that I've saved for years, a California psychologist struggling with her book manuscript wondered how she ever believed she could complete her task. She felt incompetent, foolish, "desolate." She wrote, "I've been so focused on what others might think that I've forgotten about the meaning of my writing to me." In Colorado, I listened to a quiet, wise English professor and writer describe the months of his sabbatical and how he couldn't complete the project he'd proposed to his colleagues. He became reluctant to even see them and felt like a sham since he taught writing and yet couldn't perform this complex act himself. He talked about his self-doubts, his "grief."

You bring special gifts to the planet, gifts uniquely yours, linked to your individual experiences, education, history. So how do we begin Practice 1, to value our creative self? We exercise: We exercise the courage to value our talents. As in much of life, faith is a good place to start, in this case, faith in our capacities to enrich the world. For such important work, we need time, a welcoming place, and, ideally, friends who believe in that imaginative part of ourselves. "Time? Time in *my* busy life?" Yes, time.

"But I'm afraid of trying and failing. Maybe I'm not that clever. I need to grade papers, do a load of wash, change the car oil, make supper. Anyway, people will think it's silly." We all have excuses— children, jealous partners, unsupportive parents, to-do lists, and lethargy. The most persistent challenge: the doubting voice within, the audible frowns of our face in the mirror. All of us around the world who choose or are compelled to write, paint, discover cures for deadly illnesses, or compose a song, take a risk. We leap.

Sometimes, when I teach a writing workshop to adults, I distribute small boxes of Guatemalan worry dolls and ask my students to lay out the dolls and privately name their writing worries, to confront their fears. "What if I hurt someone I write about?" "What if

I discover I'm kidding myself and I can't really write?" "I'm afraid I'm dull and won't have good ideas."

What are your fears? Would it help to name them, write them down, and then push on? Journal writing as you read this book might help. Journals allow us to hear our inside self and years later provide a window back to our younger selves. With friends or colleagues, you could also start a bookjoy club or creativity loop or circle (the book has many circles) and do the suggested exploring and writing together. Sharing, bonding—and munching—we sometimes become braver.

Bored by my whining, I now have an idea journal, a place to paste images, quotations, and thoughts that appeal to me rather than dwelling on my woes. Writer and educator Donald Murray suggests a "daybook." Devise a system that appeals to you and prompts ideas that lure you to the page, canvass, clay, yarn.

Although, like my mom, I'd always enjoyed making a nest for my family and me, a place with some visual delights, I didn't realize then the value of designing a space to nurture my creative impulses. My home revealed what mattered to me—family photos, books, a cheerful kitchen, houseplants, light. Our surroundings, our reminders, help shape us, reveal much about us if we step back and study what we've chosen, says Professor Clare Cooper Marcus, author of *House as a Mirror of Self*. Unconsciously, we may be re-creating what comforted us or rejecting what was painful.

Look around. What messages have you left for yourself in the places where you do your most inventive work? Is it at your office, desk, kitchen, garden? How are you nudging yourself in the directions you want to be moving?

How I spend my time tells me what matters in my life. Examining my daily habits, I see the choices I'm making. Then I can ask, "What are the practices I want to develop?"

I typed my first collection of rhyming poems on the gray, portable typewriter my parents gave me when I graduated from eighth grade. Years later, my writing life as an adult began on a dining-room table. I have a tidy side, but I tend to write in clutter with dictionaries—English and Spanish—books, articles scattered around, working my way through the mess of ideas and notes. I need space. When I began making time for writing, I'd sit at the table and feel awkward, foolish. What made me think I had anything to say and that anyone would want to read my thoughts and creations? I love the mystery of writing, and part of the mystery will always be how and why I stayed faithful to the work. Expect that awkward feeling, and firmly, kindly, and with a touch of humor, pull (drag) yourself along as you did the first day of college or of a new job. Be affirming. Pat yourself on the back. If we want to develop our full selves, this isn't really optional work. It's essential.

Writers write where they can, unwilling to wait for the perfect spot or for a sizzling bolt of inspiration. Although I've written at airports, in hotel rooms, and in restaurants, when possible, I now try to find a space that lures me to want to write, that sustains me a bit. I agree with Virginia Woolf on the value of "a room of one's own," but it's a luxury we don't always have, even those of us with many luxuries. Ours is often a noisy, violent world. Advertising and films can trivialize us, portray us, particularly women, as mere consumers or manikins. It takes work to remember the challenge of being human and extra work to believe we're unique. Retreating to a space that nurtures our good spirit assists our imagination to surface. I keep a few bears around—not the breathing, furry ones but figurines to remind me of the importance of hibernation. I'm often too busy, or believe I'm too busy, completing my endless list of tasks to retreat enough to hear my deeper self, to burrow in. I have to practice, intrigued by possibilities, by what I learn from writing

Design a special place, dear teacher, a welcoming place, even just a comfortable corner in a room or a desk or a table to foster your creative self, a tiny haven. Leave symbols that matter to you: rocks, pinecones, bird feathers, dried flowers, shells, whatever invites you to pause and ponder. Make regular appointments to savor time there. See your space as a work in progress (as we all are). Add to this private place—a photo, a saying, a book of photography. By shaping our space, in a small way, we nurture our creativity, our inner voice. Georgia O'Keeffe, who painted the objects she collected and studied—shells, rocks, bones—said, "I have used these things to say what is to me the wideness and wonder of the world as I live in it." How do we keep that sense of wonder as fresh as it is for a child?

The habit or discipline of regular time for exploring this imaginative part of ourselves, of persistently connecting and reconnecting with our inside self, yields rewards. When I began making time for writing in my life, I was working full-time as a university administrator and was "Mom" to my three children. Because helping them with homework and enjoying our dinners together were important to me, I began by setting aside the time I could, two to three hours on the weekend, for sitting still with books, paper, and a typewriter—my precomputer life—making time to develop my skills. The custom of valuing our inner selves begins to shape our week and our self-perception.

In one sense, no one will care much if we don't write or paint. Our internal yearning or curiosity is the medium in which we plant our hopes and our desire to develop our full, complex selves. You and I are seeking to let our voices and talents unfold. Tending required. Develop the daily and weekly habits that are quiet reminders. If it's writing you wish to explore, read, yes, for pleasure, but also read to experience fine writing. Thinking of you, I'm reading about creativity, gardens, teaching, diversity, and rereading *Gifts from the Sea.*

Unleash your curiosity and enthusiasm. We all need guides, teachers, master craft artists. When I choose my reading wisely, the possibilities excite me and bring me back to the page just as supportive readers of all ages do. Find the artists in your chosen medium, be it dance, sculpture, science, or education, who dazzle you. Float on that excitement into your own work.

I still remember the El Paso summer afternoon in 1981, when I opened an envelope and read that someone in Ohio wanted to publish one of my poems—my first publication. Such moments counter the rejections, the waiting. And there's the zing of excitement that writing can bring. When I'm working on a book, my day feels different. I notice details—sounds, faces, stories. Everything matters more—or maybe, the trivial, the petty, matters less—because I'm looking and listening for threads I can lace through the book. I'm more alert, more awake. Writing daily to you is having the same effect.

"When do you feel most alive?" asked Polly, an anthropologist. She had a small studio built behind her house to return to painting, work that brought her energy and joy. Young students often ask if I ever feel lonely when I write. Quite the contrary. Perhaps because I didn't spend time writing for many years, I feel as if I'm playing hooky when I've managed to make the quiet and space, internal and external, to explore with a pen or a keyboard.

When do *you* feel most alive?

Spend time with people who value your dream. As the wise Sufi poet Rumi wrote, "Be with those who help your being." Through the years, friends' faith has helped me more than they'll ever know. In a journal entry from my late thirties, when I was feeling discouraged about choosing to write, I jotted that my dear North Carolina friend

Elizabeth in one of our infrequent but long conversations asked, "But don't you see this is part of you? You've let your organized side dominate. Now you must let the other side catch up." I continued writing but months later wrote, "The writing has improved though I still feel very funny about doing it." Find good guides and friends who cheer on your risks and dreams.

I treasure a greeting card from a librarian in Neenah, Wisconsin, in which a green seed sends down a root, then opens—and a bird flies out. Above the drawing is a Hebrew proverb, "As is the gardener, such is the garden." How do we assist the surprise of emerging? When we value our inventive side, we release the self too often burdened by duty and thus ignored. By developing our inventive talents, we hear ourselves—explore, stretch, live more fully, and teach more effectively.

Cada cabeza es un mundo a Spanish *dicho,* says. A world exists in every head, a one-of-a-kind world. You can write, paint, dance, or compose a collage in a unique way. Your way.

In his evocative memoir, *The Names,* N. Scott Momaday, describing his mother wrote one of my favorite sentences in contemporary America literature: "She imagined who she was." Momaday goes on to say that this same imaginative act was important in his own life. Are you and I imagining who we could be and letting that *act of the imagination* expand and deepen our sense of self?

One spring, my Cincinnati gardening friend Jane, who had lived in her home for years, decided to whack back a huge honeysuckle. To her surprise, in the undergrowth, she discovered a lilac bush stunted in the shade of the huge vine. Thanks to her pruning, the lilac now had space and sun. With her attention, it began to grow—and grow. The lilac thrived, climbed, bloomed. Eventually, the bush stretched to fifteen feet.

Think of that lilac perfuming the world. What a loss if it had it not flourished. Makes me think of some of our students. In my next letter, I'll send some thoughts on the pupils we care so much about, but today I want to focus on you. Rich with meaning, powerful reminders, symbols—flowers, hearts, flags, menorahs, apples— evoke and motivate. I send you the first of my imaginary gifts: seeds. I'll put some by me, too, as symbols for the inventive hopes and dreams locked within us, waiting for us to allow a space for them, to nurture our possibilities. With the right environment, earth's magic: slowly, seeds sprout. Plenty of life energy in that small, one-syllable word: *sprout.*

Celebrating beginnings together, let's practice valuing our unique selves. Gie, a wise Swedish neighbor and friend who spoke five languages, regularly reminded me that within us we carry inner wisdom. She certainly did. The spaces we shape externally and internally, the habits we develop to put ourselves in the company of what inspires us, help us envision what we might otherwise ignore. To help you think about your personal and professional artistic work, I send optional explorations and invitations to write. You, of course, may choose to respond by painting or writing a song or revising your garden.

Joy, dear teacher! Joy!

Exploration

First, relax. Take some deep breaths. Let go of the thinking process, and let the images come. You know how we stretch (or are supposed to) before we exercise? These explorations can help you limber up too. Draw or design a collage of your ideal space for creating. I certainly can't draw well, but I find that doodling can loosen my imagination. Just play and avoid being judgmental. This exploration is just for you. Let your curiosity carry you along.

When you're ready to switch to another opportunity to see yourself on the page, sketch your sprouting self. You can do this with pencil, pen, colors, clay. You're in charge. Play!

Years ago, I spoke at a session of a program called SEED that promoted faculty book groups. Training was provided to a school leader as I remember. The books were to be written by authors of varying ethnicities, particularly those represented at the school. Might that be an idea at your campus? An interested group could select all kinds of books—children's, young adult (YA), adult fiction, and nonfiction. Perhaps using the model of One City, One Book, you would enjoy creating a One School or One Library or One Department/One Book. I remember a city version that chose a theme and then an adult, YA, and children's book connected to the theme.

Invitation to Write

Educators are fine writers. I know from the workshops I've led. Using first person, write a paragraph or more describing yourself as the lilac bush. What tangles, what doubts, and what fears have kept you from the work you'd like to do as a person, writer/artist, teacher?

Write about a path or street that you walked often as a child, giving special attention to sensory detail. Where are you? What do you see and hear? Do you smell anything appealing? How did you feel back then? Gather the details and use them to create the mood of your piece.

Value Each Student's Creative Talents

Dear Teacher,

Though we're adults (much of the time) with the psychological protection that degrees, a middle-class life, and adulthood provide, it can often be hard to value our creative selves. How much harder is it then for our students who may not have such protections and who may not see positive depictions of people like them in the world around them? Educators are incredibly important people; you change lives. How do we make the necessary time, space, and support to guide a student to value her creativity? How do we see his inventive capacities and assist him to develop them? A key strategy is through establishing a personal connection.

Committed librarians and teachers who work with young people are optimists: You invest a good part of your life, your talents, and your enthusiasm in the next generation. What energy is required! I'm reminded what hard work teaching is when I visit a campus, reality therapy. My time as a teacher from working with little ones to teaching graduate students and now my author visits and campus presentations remind me of what many don't understand, those who think teachers have it easy because they have summers off. We have principal-for-a-day programs; how about having a teacher-for-a-day? You'd need to be standing by with oxygen and vitamins to provide emergency assistance to those struggling to be inspiring, patient, knowledgeable educators—hour after hour. Why is such important work often undervalued?

A father from Mexico brings his child to the first day of school. "I give you my son," he says respectfully to the teacher. What trust. What does that child who may not understand the conversation feel surrounded by a strange language? What would you feel? What did that teacher feel I wonder?

Purposely, I ask what would you *feel* rather than what would you think because our linear, pragmatic, production-focused society often ignores the rich emotional capacities that we share. Our feelings can be resources not only for our creative endeavors but also for assisting us to understand a fellow human of whatever age, ethnicity, or gender, for assisting us in the art of teaching.

We're moved by the directness and simplicity of the father's statement. Consciously or unconsciously, parents of young ones do give us their child for much of the year. Many of us remember how that felt in our parenting years. Would this year's teacher or teachers value our child and realize just how special he was? We can be so intensely interested in a school our child attends.

Students arrive the first day of class whether in kindergarten or in a graduate course submitting, some more willingly than others, to our rules and judgments. Many dedicated educators tend to look back on all the missed opportunities for connecting with students. I do. We can apply Thornton Wilder's words from *Our Town* to our teaching life as well as to all aspects of our past: "So *all* that was going on and we never noticed!"

Master gardeners and master teachers know: possibilities—if the spark within hasn't been crushed, if the right growing conditions can be cultivated. Because we know students need to develop their inventive selves, we can connect with them, listen to and honor their stories, create time and a welcoming place as we encourage them to value and release their imaginations, as we affirm their specific talents and offer our helpful support.

You can't change school architecture reflecting societal values at a particular time in history nor change the locations of walls, windows, or doors; but you can design spaces for learning in which students see information, ideas, their interests, books, and people like them succeeding in the posters or video clips we share, the speakers we invite, the texts we assign. You can give each student a precious gift, your faith. I think of Patricia, a fine Texas teacher who referred to her third graders, many from low-income homes, as "scholars" and treated them as such. They prepared for my author visit with such thoroughness that I think they knew more about me than I did.

Year by year, we learn—from our students, their families, our colleagues, and books. And we learn by observing our responses critically, the Buddhist notion of "right seeing." What prejudices, some learned at home and some reinforced by the media, are barriers to our treating every student with dignity?

What do I see in the mirror? My many selves? Can I ever see myself without the filters I've been taught to value like youth and slimness? As I struggle to know myself, I also strive to see, really see, each student, her potential. Unfortunately, no cardboard disposable glasses exist that let us see our students without filters to remove attitudes we've absorbed as the earth absorbs toxins.

In a psychological sense, societies project their "shadows" on groups viewed as peripheral or inferior. Traits we repress, though harbor in varying degrees, we attribute to "those people," ones not like us who, in our opinion, may be too close to their families or display their emotions too openly. Jung's notion of the shadow fascinates me. He proposed that the shadow could be a place of great energy and creativity if acknowledged and incorporated wisely. As a national community, do we in overt and subtle ways seek to repress certain groups, to keep them from the spotlight of positive attention?

Overcoming stereotypes is a lifelong struggle. Sometimes we soothe our egos by deeming some folks second-class and, thus, elevating ourselves. Our egos beam. We can be so smug, so prideful. Looking down on others because of their accent, weight, wardrobe, or poverty, we comfort our fragile selves, but oh the price to a student or a fellow teacher or staff member. With a look, remark, or comment on a paper, a teacher can describe specific strengths or wound through insults. I think of the rigid art teacher who snuffed my son's interest in drawing; of the bright, young Vietnamese woman reluctant to return to college because a professor haughtily suggested she didn't belong in the pharmacy program. She's haunted by his voice, the possibility of failure.

So what do bright students—and leaders—look like? Sound like? How do we overcome the images that seep into us and shape us more than we realize? In countless media presentations, we see certain groups as articulate citizens and other groups as problems. Our country is now referred to as the "world nation" because we're home to complex cultures, languages, and religions. Some schools offer opportunities to interact and learn from a wide variety of families, ticketless travel if we see diversity as an opportunity. Negative attitudes can be so deeply entrenched, though, that, sadly, some teachers aren't excited at the opportunities to teach and learn from those not like them.

Such teachers are a minority, I trust, and because of strong teacher and librarian preparation programs, new educators care about all their students rather than only about upper- and middle-class students who might fit a past image of an ideal student. Dick and Jane never did represent all of America's children. In fact, if we look at our national history, phrases such as "typical American experience" may refer to the immigrant experience. Our legacies are complex, and our families have varying stories to add.

In this nation of immigrants, schools and communities respond differently to the increase in students from Asia and Latin America who experience the discrimination and resentment once felt by the Irish and Germans who came here, also bringing their hopes and dreams. Years ago, anthropologist Edward Hall wrote astutely about how unaware we are of the profound way we're all shaped by culture, how we in the U.S. often view foreigners as "underdeveloped Americans." Sadly, this perspective isn't only applied to foreigners. Does your local school district view its significant educational challenges as a nuisance, or does it believe that every student and family matters equally?

Immigrant students enter at all levels often lacking the English skills and, at times, the study skills to succeed. What does it feel like to be a Spanish- or Mandarin-speaking student in a school in which no staff member speaks your home language? A parent wrote me, "In this country, my language cannot protect my children." Can we feel that mother's sorrow and worry? Many of us can think of the generation in our own family that went to bed with those sighs, heartaches, and fears. How do we help our students to understand the wise Spanish *dicho, El que habla dos lenguas, vale por dos.* If you speak two languages, you count twice.

Parents like the speaker in my poem "Elena," who feel isolated, who secretly practice English so they can be of use to their children attending our high schools, display great courage. I wrote the sad, found poem "Learning English: Chorus in Many Languages," inspired by the letters from teens and adults struggling to learn English who write me after reading "Elena." I incorporated their words and grief.

I am embarrassed
almost every day
why people so mean. . . .

people still laugh at me
when words stumble out
I want to disappear. . . .

My Own True Name

Educators often regret that they can't communicate with all their students and families in their native language. Such educators long to know more about other cultures too. Although such knowledge is a great asset, it's our attitude that's most important. I watched in admiration as Anne, a school librarian, greeted each student as she would a guest in her home. I admired her determination to begin the relationship building by striving to pronounce each student's name correctly knowing the power of her own name in her life. Eva Hoffman, in her illuminating memoir *Lost in Translation: A Life in a New Language,* remembers the pain of hearing her name changed to suit her school. Hoffman writes of the "names that make us strangers to ourselves."

In some schools, Eduardo and his family the Garcias will have their culture and home language valued. He'll be assessed to make teaching him more effective, but no judgment will be passed that connects his worth with his family's bank account or ability to speak English. Effective teachers resist teaching to a test but have always engaged in relevant assessment. Talented educators who hone the gift of making connections, respectful of every student, have transformative powers. Sadly, at some schools and in some classrooms, Eduardo and his family will be viewed as burdens.

What a challenge to create learning communities that counter, alter existing prejudices that students early grasp and internalize. I met with a group of Oklahoma high school students in their library to discuss poetry. Some were Latino students, and though not all may have spoken Spanish, some did. I read my poem, "Elena," that has the line *Vamos a pedirle dulces a mamá. Vamos.*

"What do the words mean in Spanish?" I asked. Silence. Some students avoided eye contact though they knew the answer. "Let's go ask Mom for candy. Let's." In middle and high schools and even in colleges, students are often reluctant to say what they know. A sad irony. In an institution founded to educate and inspire, students had knowledge to share, linguistic knowledge, but they felt unsafe speaking up. What they know is stigmatized. As a Colorado university student said, "We just care too much about what other people think."

Objectively, we know that each language is a rich, complex system, but if we're candid, we know that we're influenced by language hierarchies. A British accent can signal "proper" manners, French accent— sophistication, Italian accent—strong emotions *and* good cooking, Spanish accent—for some, mental laziness. And how do people from other countries view our U.S. English and view us? Stereotypes are taught. In subtle ways, is your school continuing to teach them or countering them? It's a myth that we can be neutral in this work.

People who struggle to learn another language and people interested in languages and communication know that no language is inferior. It holds and reveals human ingenuity. And yet a fellow speaker at a Virginia children's literature conference said that Spanish was a "simpler language," that while English offered many synonyms for *red,* for example, Spanish offered limited choices. Did she believe such misinformation?

Native language is intimately tied to our identity. It's our inside voice. In 1996, Estafanita Martinez, at that time in her eighties, was honored as a "Living Treasure" in New Mexico. Spanked as a child for speaking Tewa, one of the few remaining Tewa speakers, she worked with professors to preserve her language and utilized it in storytelling. She remembered the power of her native language when she was little. "That was the only language in which you could really put your thoughts across to your little friends," she said.

We and our students bring unquestioned presumptions about one another into the classroom. "Until we understand the assumptions in which we are drenched, we cannot know ourselves," writes poet Adrienne Rich. Some students arrive full of self-confidence and others lug heavy doubts. Many students have trouble relating to literature in their textbooks when it doesn't reflect their lives, when it fails to reflect our rich diversity. Students can reach erroneous conclusions. "Those people who write those poems," said a Latino student, "must have bigger brains. People like me couldn't write that." He probably doesn't know the *dicho,* the saying, in Spanish: *Nadie nace enseñado.* No one is born educated. If we believe our national rhetoric, and if we believe in the power of education, how can we settle for anything less than truly equal educational opportunity for all, which includes affirming each student's creative potential?

As we practice nourishing our imagination, we can more critically assess our strategies to nurture student work. High expectations honor students, say that we believe they can achieve. We become discouraged and even angry with peers who judge capacities based on skin color, ethnicity, accent, gender, religion. Poverty is a way to categorize people too, of course. As my friend Patricia wisely observes, "In this country being poor is a crime."

As we guide our students to value their inventive talents, an internal habit, we can shape places that externally support their creative and educational journey. What we call American literature is becoming far more interesting for all age groups as we savor and explore our national and hemispheric cultural wealth. It offers students a wide assortment of voices and images. When students see their teacher excited about books that include families and homes like theirs, they connect more deeply with themselves, with us, and with text.

Some are blessed with families who can work with them on their reading and writing, but in our diverse democracy, we have students whose parents may not read text themselves or who may not read or speak English though they may read the world wisely and have survival stories and oral linguistic wealth to share. We can foster a literacy legacy that doesn't exist in some families by our example, by asking a student in first grade or graduate school questions about her life and dreams, listening to her stories and ideas, and assisting her to draw and write her unique tales. From personal experience, we know that bringing the inside voice or image out into the world requires effort and some faith in ourselves and in the process. Because of previous educational experiences, poor skills, or weak self-image, many students need us to nurture their courage, to en*courage* them to bring themselves to the canvass or page.

Although teaching can include lecturing, isn't it really about establishing connections: between ideas, theories, thinkers, texts, teacher and student? We won't always succeed, of course, but not to try is to cheat both our students and ourselves. We will learn less and, in some ways, be less. Knowing that younger students are constructing their identity, how do we create a welcoming and psychologically safe place for linguistic exploration? Laurie, a visual artist from Kentucky, recently told me, "I remember two teachers. One was a high school English teacher, and I didn't give a hoot about English. The other was a college history teacher, and I didn't care that much about it either. They were both so passionate though. They made me want to learn, and I didn't feel so dumb. I felt I *could* learn."

What wonderful teachers do you remember? And what not-so-wonderful ones?

I cringe remembering the writing professor in Wisconsin who reminded her students of the first grade she received on a writing paper in college. "*W* for worthless," her professor said. She told the students that the remark silenced her for years and that even though she had published a poetry collection, "In the back of my mind, I can sometimes still hear that voice." Our quiet teacher voices can echo for years.

Deep inside, educators want to be remembered. Daily, you're investing in the future, preparing the next generation to make the world a better, more just place. Good teaching is an art. Braiding your own inventive talents with your art of teaching enriches both.

By affirming each student through a personal connection, opportunities for unique possibilities surface, and we can guide him to value himself and his inventiveness. Large classes, emphasis on standardized tests for nonstandardized students, time constraints, and stereotypes pose challenges as do national skepticism about teacher preparation, educational politics, and budget crises.

Let's think of the seeds I sent. Nature can't be totally standardized, thank heavens. As we practice valuing our creative selves, dear teacher, we connect with a complex part of ourselves and better understand the fears and doubts students bring to the blank page. We see and feel differently if we're diving deeply enough into our work, into our humanity.

Theoretically, at schools and universities, students and faculty participate in exciting and respectful intellectual inquiry, the practice of mutual learning. But writing is a private act that, in our school years, we perform in public places for a grade. We ask students to reveal themselves to us, to share their dreams and opinions and fears while proving their mastery of writing conventions. Some of the finest teachers I know are willing to make themselves vulnerable, to reveal their doubts and histories so that students can follow their lead.

In *The Botany of Desire,* biologist Michael Pollan has a section on the domesticated apple: *Malus domestica.* The ancestor of our cherished apple is a wild apple from Kazakhstan in West Asia. Apples, then, as in "American as apple pie" and those shiny globes often given to teachers, like many of us, are of migrant stock. Like apples, our ancestors learned to flourish here and to nourish and sweeten the place.

Seeds of promise. When we respect our students and the good that they bring and when we share literature that reflects their realities and many other realities, students find a place for their creative selves in language and in languages. They are liberated to bring all of themselves to the classroom. With your guidance, they can then connect to the world's literary heritage. What a gift, a place in which each is welcome and in which each voice adds to the chorus.

One Sunday morning, walking on Boylston Street in Boston, I went inside beautiful Old South Church "gathered in 1669." I like to slip unnoticed into places defined as holy. I was in luck. Since the choir was practicing, I sat and watched an amazingly energetic choir director with his group of various shapes, colors, and ages. He asked them to go to the back of the church and practice their entrance. In they filed solemnly, and then suddenly they did a little dance step. They kept entering, singing, and interspersing the dance step, and eventually, they started resoundingly clapping their rhythm. The room was transformed by a traditional Cameroon melody and by the singers' spirits. "Here I am in traditional Boston," I thought, "at a famous historical church, watching a director whose excitement energizes everyone involved and alters the very air." The music I enjoyed that Sunday was made by a diverse group's required practice and a director listening to every voice, realizing the power of each individual and the power of the whole.

Tips

To encourage your students to talk about their questions and work, share some challenges or details in your creative process.

Invite your students to design a creativity corner or space.

Exploration for You

Focusing on positive memories, think of a memorable teacher. What made her or him so effective? In what ways are you like or unlike her or him? In your journal, answer the following question: How do I wish to be remembered by my students, their families, the staff, and my peers?

Invitation to Write

Gather memories of a favorite teacher. Make a list of details, either the sounds, gestures, or objects that defined that person. What did she wear? How did he walk? What do you think she ate for breakfast? What did he read at night? Write at least one poem about a memorable teacher in your present voice or in the voice of your younger self. Express the emotion through the concrete.

The following poem was inspired by a graduate student and literacy advocate Paulina Moreno, who was born in Mexico and educated in California. I wrote the poem for the first Elementary Education Graduating Class at North Carolina State University.

My Turn

My first-grade teacher's frowns taught me
I was welcome as a fly and dull as dirt.
For one long year, timidly, I'd raise my hand
and feel the sting of her brown eyes.

Welcome as a fly and dull as dirt.
Why didn't she see the smart me?
I'd feel the sting of my tall teacher's eyes.
I frowned at my face in the mirror.

The next year, Mrs. Hassan saw the real me.
Her laugh floated, like bubbles, and we floated too.
I'd look at the changing face in my mirror.
We read, sang songs I still sing. I sparkled.

I still float on Mrs. Hassan's bubbly laugh.
She wrote me a poem, taught me I was special.
Now it's my turn, in each child, to see their spark.
Like all the Mrs. Hassans, I'll help the glow grow.

CHAPTER TWO

Enjoy Quiet

Dear Teacher,

Are you familiar with labyrinths, not the Greek labyrinth of the Minotaur, but the spiral paths for walking and meditation? I first became aware of them when my husband and I visited majestic Chartres Cathedral outside of Paris. Travel teaches patience, a valuable trait for a writer. We'd been assured that even with my very limited French securing tickets on the correct train would be no problem, but we watched the first train roll down the tracks without us.

Eventually, we arrived in Chartres and walked up to the imposing gray stone church. Much within interested us, including the rose window, but we were disappointed to the see the famous marble labyrinth at the nave of the church covered by chairs. Dating back to 1235, this most famous early Christian style labyrinth designed in symmetry with the rose window, is thought to have been symbolic of pilgrimages to Jerusalem, symbolic of life's journey and salvation. Labyrinths have gone in and out of fashion.

Like dutiful tourists, we bought postcards and booklets about the labyrinth that December, wandered the windy, cobbled streets of Chartres, and were relieved to be on the correct train heading to Paris at the end of the day. I'm sharing four labyrinth stories because walking the circular paths is a way to practice entering quiet, a habit necessary for interior travels and for inventive thinking. "Go into yourself," advised the poet Rilke in *Letters to a Young Poet,* a book I love. Do you feel comfortable with quiet, alone without the frenzy of activity? Does seeking, finding, and savoring quiet appeal to you?

In part, academics, researchers, artists, readers do what they do in the necessary silence to be their most imaginative. Once sinking into stillness becomes a habit, it feels refreshing as water.

I've learned the importance of cultivating time for reflection along with the intentional habits of making the time and space to value our creative self. It's hard enough to hear our internal voice without asking it to compete with big or small screens, distracting music, family requests, e-mails. In developing the habit of the inward journey, we take the risk of leaving our surface selves for a bit, the persona with which we face the world, and exploring what we really think, feel, fear, our deeper waters, the well of the self. Poet Seamus Heaney reminds us that poetry is "earned with silences," as are wisdom and insights. We need quiet both when we work and in preparation for our best work. Rabbi Nachman's prayer about enjoying the outdoors begins, "Grant me the ability to be alone." Mulling time, pondering time, what I do when I imagine a new phase of my garden or begin to imagine a new book.

A few years after seeing Chartres, on a visit to San Francisco, I was delighted to walk two labyrinths at Grace Cathedral. At the outdoor labyrinth, I enjoyed watching people stretch with great concentration in the movements of Tai Chi. Our rituals can exercise us physically, mentally, emotionally, and spiritually. I scribbled notes on the labyrinth concept and pattern, the journey, a metaphor that appeals to me perhaps because I travel often. Labyrinths, unlike mazes, aren't puzzles. They can be habits like attending a place of worship, meditating, eating or abstaining from certain foods, gathering for family celebrations.

My friend Elizabeth, who shares my interest in this meditating tradition, ordered a canvass labyrinth for the students to walk at her North Carolina campus. When she came to Santa Fe for a visit, we went to lectures at a nearby museum on both the history and the spiritual aspects of the design. Soon after, I met with Kate, a young gardener, for advice on our very small garden. I casually asked if we could add a tiny labyrinth made of rocks strictly for viewing, I stressed, a reminder of the value of quiet and reflection in our busy lives.

"Let's just put in a little labyrinth," bold Kate proposed.

I stared at the space we had to play with since the garden consisted of a dark-brown wooden deck and a wide, curving gravel path with flagstone edging. Flowerbeds, always needing more work, bordered the path.

"You want to put a tiny labyrinth in the largest flower bed?" I asked confused. I could see the existing borders and was visualizing within them. Kate extended her right arm in a wide arc. "Forget the path and the borders," she said. "We can remove all that and use the available space for the labyrinth. I mean, why have one if you can't walk it?"

I was struck and remain struck at how limited my perspective had been. How often do I let my perceptions and assumptions limit my possibilities? How often do I see moveable borders as fixed? You can well imagine where thoughts about moveable borders took me. Born on the U.S.-Mexico border, I've thought and written often about the physical border, about other separations, and I used the word "borders" as the title of an early poetry collection. Whether we're talking about garden borders or borders based on class, language, religion, or culture, how often do we see them as rigid?

My husband and I began to remove the flagstone edging. The task, like most house projects, was more difficult than we imagined. Because some of the flagstone was set in concrete, we needed considerable energy and a large shovel to loosen the rock. As we worked an area, scraping the dirt and rocks from the sides of the pink stone, we were surprised to see that only about a fourth of the stone was visible above the surface. The deep trench made by the previous owners held the border secure. And isn't that true of us, dear teacher? The borders we inherit are deep. Then we carefully hide the depths of the stubborn and arbitrary divisions from our fellow humans that we continue to assume, the lines we draw or accept and live within.

The conversation with Kate also reminded me of the value of planning with people who are different from us but who know the terrain in which we hope to be creative at home or at school. Kate knew the soil, the irrigation system that would conserve the most water, the plants that could flourish in the dry shade the garden offered. I've enjoyed gardening since my twenties but had usually worked in low desert and had received advice and cuttings from friends and relatives who knew what would thrive in El Paso. Dry shade posed new challenges. I became acquainted with coralbells and hardy plumbago. Kate helped guide how I spent my gardening time, money, energy.

When the borders and wide gravel path were removed, we were ready for the garden transformation, the creation of new patterns. The garden area looked bigger, a space of possibilities, fallow, totally different without neat, predictable boundaries. Curious sparrows and blue jays came to inspect. Hummingbirds darted through looking for the familiar flowers now in plastic bags in a corner.

The following morning, we took a final glance at pictures of labyrinths shaped as concentric circles, squares, octagonals. With

Kate, we selected a small, simple pattern technically referred to as the classic pattern though ours would have fewer rings, suited to our space. We liked the idea of adapting a model to the space available, a life lesson. As a desert lover and a lover of Mexican culture, I was also intrigued by letting a Mexican, high-desert garden labyrinth evolve.

Kate described where she planned to put the small spiral paths, but I still couldn't imagine how even a diminutive labyrinth would fit in the allotted space. Writing teaches trust, though. After years of approaching blank pages full of hope and persistence, I've learned to practice faith. (And I now live in *Santa Fe,* words meaning holy faith.) We knew we'd learn as we explored and that, like it or not, we'd make adjustments, practice revision.

Why a labyrinth I kept asking myself? I like to walk, my feet not on concrete but on the earth. I understand articles about nature a healer, about how being outdoors reduces stress; ecopsychology, the connection between our wellness and our relationship with our world. When I walk alone, the rhythm helps me journey inside. Also, I want to live a more meditative life. Busyness can be shallow and superficial, yet, as I heard educator Donald Graves observe, many of us equate it with health. "I'm so busy" as "I'm so productive, so well."

In your busy days, do you yearn for more internal peace? I liked the notion of walking the earth rings slowly and pondering, of consciously choosing to be reflective, if only for a short time. I thought of monks of various religions around the world pacing and meditating. No structured plan is necessary, of course, but when I began reading about labyrinths, I liked the metaphor—entering the spiral paths as a private journey, moving from the external world to our internal space. People sometimes enter labyrinths with a question, hoping the rotational rhythm of quiet winding will help them shed the cares and details, the naggings and natterings that fill their minds. At the center, the core of the path (sometimes called a rosette), the walker pauses, perhaps, for an insight or to stop in solitude at the heart of this intentional mulling. It's like a circular walk deeper into myself, a brief hibernation or incubation.

To mark that pausing place in the garden's concentric circles, we placed a large, glazed blue ceramic pot with a small pump to send water over some desert rocks. I thought of the privacy of Islamic gardens in their arid terrains that with elaborate pools and fountains emphasize water, its beauty, its sacredness, the garden as paradise.

. . . . the fabled gardens

of Persia. . . .

Water sings crystal

flights in fountains,

streams tile-lined canals into white

petaled breaths: orange blossoms,

jasmine, into scarlet

incense, roses coiling

their velvet spell.

"Oasis," *Agua Santa: Holy Water*

The water caught light and its splashing sound refreshed the visitor as we hoped the tiny *arroyo azul* beneath the blue sky would soothe and cool all who paused there. We need quiet to hear the music of the earth and to hear the music we uniquely bring to the earth.

The cyclical walk would slow me down, help me focus on my work. The meditation theory is that, when ready, the walker slowly winds her way out to rejoin her community, a calmer self. With luck, she brings a small epiphany, a good idea. People walk the rings for varying reasons, of course, for relaxation, focus, making space for creativity.

I continued reading about this tradition, savoring the reflective aspect and the photographs. The earliest surviving designs found in many parts of the world, in cultures including Native American culture, are rock carvings and cave paintings, some dating from 2000 BC. The design later appears on coins, clay tablets, pottery. Difficult to date, the tradition of path labyrinths seems popular by the medieval period in Scandinavia, England, and Germany, among other places. The number of rings varies as do designs and materials—hedge, stone, and turf. I smiled at the commercialism of some of the Web sites on the topic, at the pins, cards, key rings, CDs, newsletters. You can have an online labyrinth experience complete with music. Catalogs offer hand-sized labyrinths that a person can trace with a finger or wooden stick. Labyrinths have also become popular at schools and occasions for peace gatherings. Some writers on labyrinths associate the design with a seashell, others with a spider's web. I like that web notion too, the complex way we are all connected.

Kate used our garden hose to illustrate how the paths would wind. The borders so recently in place began to fade from our memories. With picks and shovels, the garden trio carved and dug, creating a single winding path.

By the end of the day, plants rested in the trenches, and birds arrived to peck seeds and hop down the paths. Small earth rings eddied out. I thought of my elementary school teacher years ago, who spoke of our impact eddying out, circles of energy moving into the world. A number of the thinkers I admire, including David Steindl-Rast, mention the need for both reflection and action to do our unique work. Time alone, solitude and not loneliness, heals and propels us.

I took notes on the process and watched Kate and her crew leave exhausted, as you often feel at the end of a day of helping students to see their world and their fellow students in new ways. We can also feel exhausted at striving to move our music or writing in new directions, an afternoon writing haiku we like, or trying to envision a totally new way to describe or draw the room we slept in when we were seven. These efforts to create can also energize us.

Each day brought progress for the young gardeners though Kate looked mighty discouraged at times. We hadn't realized that this was her first attempt to design a labyrinth. Creativity requires risk.

"Yea!" Kate finally shouted.

Young faces radiated pleasure and excitement. The pump worked, and water spilled down the tiny *arroyo*. The creation was a visual blessing. My practical side saw that this beautiful, meditative space would require work, experimenting with what to add and what to remove. The process reminded me of editing, creating paths so carefully that the reader can move along without being distracted by the unnecessary. As writers and teachers, we strive to create paths to our inner self and to others.

The previous year, I'd purchased some beautiful small, blue stones from Bali. I'd spent hours in the fall lugging them and then strewing them to simulate a stream near my stoic companion, a concrete turtle, in one of the shrub beds. Gardening is a stern teacher, and fall leaves of aspens, locust, and ash trees plus pine needles soon covered my pebbles. Time for revision. Not about to lose my investment, my stubborn self collected every stone, bagged them, and lugged them into the garage. I tell beginning writers to save what they've invested in for the future.

Although initially Kate hadn't been overly impressed with my blue treasures, she eventually decided to line the tiny dry rock bed with them. Of course, they needed a good cleaning and washing. "Beauty has its price," my mother often said.

A weary Kate left proclaiming the need for "a new perspective." I thought of how often we leave a manuscript or a school building with that same feeling. In time, my husband and I rearranged the rocks again and planned additions and changes for the following year. Gardens, unlike manuscripts, tolerate endless revisions. The bird feeders meant persistent weeding, like the plucking out of the negative internal voices that tell us we can't really write, paint, or create, that we can't really be amazing teachers who change the world. Pull those weedy thoughts out by the roots and toss them as far as you can.

I anticipated the flowers, annuals in pots on the deck and perennials in the earth rings. Commenting on Monet's art, Arsene Alexandre in the French newspaper *Le Figaro,* wrote, "Who inspired all this? His flowers. Who was his teacher? His garden."

I stared at the eddying earth windings and found unexpected comfort in their circularity. Why? Because the world is round? Because it circles the sun? Because day follows night, follows day? Because of moon beauty? Because I was curled round in my womb beginnings? Because of life cycles? Because of circles of family and hope? Even the startled exclamation, "**O!**" spins around.

I share the labyrinth stories to encourage you to find or create your quiet spots and to visit them regularly. Maybe you find quiet in walking, riding a bus or train, staring out at a vista. Do such places help you go into yourself for a bit, pondering, mulling spaces you leave refreshed and more fully yourself, a creative person, artist, teacher? Savor such places often.

We moved from the house with the small garden and labyrinth a few years ago, but I carry its peace. I smile remembering how helpful it was. When I was frustrated or irritated, I'd walk out back, look up at the blue Santa Fe sky, take some deep breaths, and walk the labyrinth. To be honest, my frustration stomps aren't usually about my writing. Our present home is surrounded by native trees and desert plants with a view that's a gift from the universe. Wise and respected poet Stanley Kunitz, who understood the connection between gardening and poetry, reminds us to "respect the land before alterations are made." Probably wise organizational advice too. Recently, inspired by paths in Japanese gardens, we planned a *caminito,* a little walking trail, "a meditation path," says our friend Murray. The desert stroll is a place to enjoy the views without being pierced by cactus, a way to walk off annoyances and to feast, be inspired by the wonder of the desert including its dramatic clouds. Bordering the path, we put playful Mexican pottery animals, a small rock labyrinth, and a stone circle, another ancient, intriguing, though mysterious, tradition.

Can you design quiet time for some mental strolling and meandering, for feeling at home with yourself and by yourself? I send you a miniature labyrinth. May it remind you of the necessary silence we need to do our internal work.

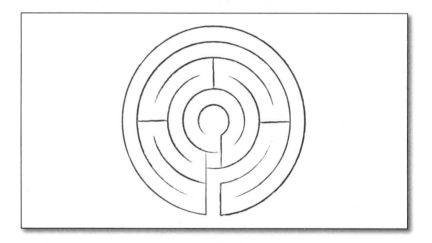

Exploration

Begin by drawing, painting, or creating a collage of yourself in a place that nurtures your solitude. Again, focus on sensory details.

Create a companion image of yourself in a quiet place you liked as a child or teenager.

Invitation to Write

Gather details about that childhood image. How old are you? How do you feel about yourself? What are you wearing? Are you alone? What do you like most about this place you remember? Writing or drawing quickly to resist your judging self, write or draw at least one paragraph/image about what you're hearing and feeling.

Create Quiet Spaces for Students

Dear Teacher,

Did you have a favorite place, a private space, when you were little? Many of us chose a quiet, outdoor space where we were alone but with a trusted adult close by. What blessings to know safe places, loving family, and the solace of quiet. How many in the world and in our own country, including fellow teachers and many students, have not received those gifts. As we discover how our creative self thrives when we make space and time for quiet, how do we help our students experience its pleasure and value?

In many homes and apartments, quiet may seem dull or a luxury. We can help students experience not the cold prescriptive educational silence of past decades but regular, welcoming, relaxed, quiet time to listen, think, plan, create. Do you enjoying reading aloud to your students, your clear voice sharing the authors you love? Are you finding books you didn't grow up with that reflect your students' lives, easing their connection to text? Once, reading to students implied little ones; now adults clamor for books on tape. We, humans of all ages, enjoy a return to the oral tradition, the music of the human voice telling us stories.

How do we help students understand the necessity of quiet to do their challenging projects and how to create such spaces for themselves? By helping them experience and, thus, develop the habit of hearing their inner selves, intrigued by their own stories and ideas. Students of all ages, for example, benefit from a few moments of quiet before drawing or writing. Invite your students to close their eyes, and in addition to reading to them, you can use music or visualizations, play a tape, or talk to them to let them settle into themselves. Do you have a memory of writing at their age that you could share with them?

Though students can learn to value quiet, media and family often pose challenges. Patricia, who now teaches future teachers, knew the value of designing reading corners at her elementary school. Because she worked with families of modest incomes, she met with parents privately to demonstrate setting up a small study and reading area at home. She didn't discuss this with a group of parents, she explained, because she didn't want anyone to feel embarrassed as they explored their options. Like Charlene, another preservice professor, and many other educators, Patricia wanted and needed parents as partners. She explored ways to collaborate with families.

Wise elementary school educators, aware of the shame parents can feel at their lack of schooling or inability to read, emphasize the parents' strengths, articulate the resources they bring: language, culture, memories, values, expectations, life experiences. Just as we talk about the need for role models for students, we need role models for parents. Without school familiarity, parents may feel they don't belong at schools or libraries, afraid of being embarrassed, of making a mistake, particularly if they don't speak English. Such parents can view school personnel as intimidating experts. Haven't we too, dear teacher, avoided places where we thought we'd feel out of place, where we might not be not dressed correctly, or know what was expected? We can be both educators with high standards and guides, advocates for the students lost in our language and ways, often our immigrant students who find our land so strange, as did so many of our grandparents or great-grandparents.

Parents who, often through no fault of their own, didn't attend school or were forced because of economic pressures to move often or to drop out early, need information presented with the same care and attention as we ideally devote to staff development. Schools now have parent specialists, councils, and leadership conferences that foster parenting skills, including creating necessary quiet.

Dedicated teachers, experienced at working with such families of limited economic resources, offer concrete suggestions. Committed principals, important educational leaders, participate in person and through newsletters, often in the families' home languages, welcoming families and reminding them often of the importance of their active participation in their children's education and of the value of public, school, class, and home libraries. Ideally, such administrators agree with writer and literacy advocate Stephen Krashen that "a print rich environment is not a luxury but a necessity."

"I tell them, 'Your child needs to see you at school,'" says Ana, a principal, but she says this as an ally. She builds a relationship based on respect and on the shared goal of caring about the children. Schools offer classes for parents that explain the school day, report cards, school goals and policies, strategies for supporting student reading, opportunities for parent participation, curriculum overviews, and the importance of setting high expectations at home in a supportive way. Teachers help parents understand the student's role and create occasions for parents to talk about their values, customs, dreams for their children.

Some schools and libraries also offer classes for parents, including English classes, literacy training, book clubs. Elementary and middle schools invite presenters of local summer programs to address students and families to explain what is available and how an unstructured summer can breed passivity that impedes student progress.

Startling and beautiful as any rose are the unsung heroines and heroes I meet in classrooms and libraries who are committed to their students and their families. These educators resist the easy judgments based on thorny old attitudes and negative media images. Some make home visits when possible. More who work with bilingual students are learning home languages. Such teachers strive to treat all moms and dads the way they treat school board members and their spouses. By working with parents, by having the young (or young at heart) connect to what they read and to what they draw or make, we help our students become comfortable with themselves and to connect with words on the page in deep and meaningful ways.

Because you and I are print rich—we have books in our homes and feel at home in books—deciphering text is one of our strengths. I was intrigued by the insight of educators Rita and Marco Portales that inexperienced readers at any age see words in a line of text as having equal weight, unaware that some words "have greater heft." The skills like learning to read that we once struggled with, we now take for granted.

"How do you advise parents who don't speak English and who may not be readers to help their little ones at home?" I ask. A bilingual teacher answers, "I tell the parents that though they may not speak English, they are needed to help their child become a good reader. Reading time should be a pleasant time, not a punishment. I ask them to have their child read aloud to them every night. I coach the parents to show interest as the child reads, praising the child, asking her to explain in Spanish (or whatever her home language is) what she read, and then asking her questions." The child is practicing the intellectual skill of being bilingual and experiencing bookjoy.

Teachers discover the energy of this work, particularly elementary school teachers who focus on the capacities of families and communities rather than on their deficits. Such educators want to learn and be transformed by the parents. Oh, the outreach work can be tiring and discouraging but also immensely invigorating.

We weren't born knowing how to foster a love of books and reading, we had good models and opportunities. Now, it's our turn to train parents as literacy coaches for other parents. My daughter visited a Philadelphia elementary school where outside each classroom was a photo of the teacher happily reading a book. Schools can create family read posters featuring the schools' families. Some family programs read picture books, including bilingual books, to the parents and then give the parents the books to take home. Parents are taught how to use the pictures to tell their child the story and to develop the habit of family conversations connected to books. At one school, students who might not have bookshelves decorated sturdy, cardboard boxes to take home as their new book place.

Of course, I understand the phrase "Good parents read to their children every night," but what about the thousands of parents of all colors, the often-ignored parents, who can't read? How do we make our language more sensitive to our national realities?

Our students are diverse in countless ways. To encourage reading and writing, educators who work with elementary school students urge all parents to share family stories and history. They urge parents to model reading and to read with their child, and urge parents literate in another language to have their child see them reading whether newspapers, magazines, recipe books. Librarians and teachers also teach parents who are not text literate new strategies. Outstanding elementary school educators share bookjoy, excited about teaching students who aren't print-rich, who haven't inherited the unearned gift of a literacy legacy that you and I enjoy. To form mutually beneficial partnerships with families, respect and concern are more essential than speaking the families' home language. We can persistently find good translators, preferably adults. Guiding requires trust. With elementary students, establishing connections with families of all economic levels and home languages yields benefits. This work can be easier when the families' circumstances are much like ours, but national teacher and student demographics differ more and more. This is true in urban and low-income areas, but it can also be true in private schools.

While watching a documentary on cartoonist Charles Schultz, I was saddened by the photographs of shy "Sparky" in Minnesota, whose parents did not frequent their only son's school because they didn't feel they'd belong. The son of this German and Norwegian couple gave us Charlie Brown. An American journey?

It's an honor to visit schools where collaborations exist with all kinds of parents and schools where principals and teachers practice a difficult silence so that others may teach and lead whether through parent councils or informal bilingual support committees for libraries, for example. Libraries anxious to involve families from diverse communities in library programming can ask Latino or Chinese families, to name but a few, what they want and need, and then they can involve them and show them that the library is truly theirs. Doing *for* others is always easier than doing *with* them, but embedded in the former is the assumption that I know best.

When I force myself to listen, I learn. Rosi, a creative university program convener, invited me to her Tucson women's group. The members spoke Spanish and faced many economic challenges, but they eloquently shared their dreams because Rosi treated the group with deep respect, perceiving their intelligence. Rather than emphasizing the learnable skills they lacked—speaking and reading English—she emphasized what they knew: their history, family experiences, cultural knowledge, resourcefulness, inventiveness. Because she spoke to them as thinkers and scholars, read and discussed literature with them, the women blossomed, shaped their group, wrote and spoke articulately about wanting to contribute to society, about strategies for aiding their children with school. Taken seriously, they took themselves seriously. A small section of the school library was set aside for them, and they savored quiet, enjoyed books, including picture books, along with their children.

Ever since Ana, an educator, once a migrant worker, told me that when she was little, she'd leave her small, noisy house in South Texas and go down by the canal to read, I've pictured her there. I imagine Antonia, who became a college historian, running to the bookmobile that came to the migrant camp in Washington State, the opportunity she credits for inspiring her to read and learn. Such educators who lived the challenges many of our students face can be our teachers and help us understand our students' realities whether in rural or urban settings, essential understanding if we're to introduce students to the pleasure and importance of quiet and how to create or find it.

Research continues to illustrate the importance of a diverse team at a hospital, in a corporation, on campus. Do we value such diversity within our faculty? More than once educators have confided, "When I was little, I didn't know we were poor." One teacher remembered reading about her neighborhood as a poor neighborhood in the newspaper. She said, "I thought, 'Are *we* poor?'" Did her colleagues know that aspect of her journey? Do we heed the varying insights in our educational community? Fellow teachers, staff, the families of our students, and community members can guide us, but can we hear and appreciate the suggestions?

What if part of the knowledge we need to do our work isn't only delivered in rooms with a podium and a lecturer or entertainer at the front? What if our potential "teacher" is a Vietnamese mom or dark-skinned grandfather who comes without the trappings of a middle-class professional—the clothes, the car, the familiarity with our controlled modes of social interaction? What if the person with valuable information is the custodian, the cafeteria cook, or a parent or grandparent new to this country? Sadly, negative images can be heard at professional meetings. "If you see cheap Mexican restaurants in your area, you want to have library books in Spanish." Groan. Luckily, the librarians and teachers I know would be horrified at this remark. The media and our own meetings and publications can reinforce a narrow image of what important teachers look and sound like.

Knowing we are all distorted by media images, that none of us is totally objective, how do we open our hearts and minds to the guides around us who may not have advanced degrees or lists of publications but who know what we need to know to connect more effectively with our students. I fear there are teachers who secretly long for other students, students who look and sound like them. Some of our students may have the same longing about their teachers. These are our students though, and not all, but many look up to us, count on us, their link to new opportunity.

Whether we're talking about garden borders or borders based on gender, class, language, religion, or culture, how often do we see them as fixed, limiting our creativity in our personal lives and in our work as teachers? How often do we let our perceptions and assumptions limit our possibilities?

"Those parents will never come."

"Those kids can never do this work."

"Those kids aren't really college material."

"How can the families help if they can't speak English?"

Perceived separations indeed separate us, and too often, we easily see the world in terms of insiders and outsiders. We've all felt on the outside. How do I remember the discomfort?

It's difficult for us to relinquish our familiar and comfortable role as teacher and to practice the owl's sage advice.

A wise old owl sat in an oak,

The more he saw, the less he spoke,

The less he spoke, the more he heard,

Why can't we all be like that wise old bird?

Anonymous wisdom

My mouth and ears can be so full of *my* opinions that I can't hear.

What is our intent, our calling, to do this hard work of being teachers and to do it well, to excel because we're excited about learning and about students, about their promise? We know the impact fine teachers had in our own lives. What do I need to know to become the teacher or librarian I want to be? Quiet assists our inventive work including our teaching. We seek to connect with our deeper selves, and in the art of teaching, we seek to connect with individual students and to support them in hearing and connecting to their inside selves, to text and, thus, to write or draw or compose music more imaginatively.

When my husband and I decided to create a labyrinth, we began with a vision. We sought help on understanding the terrain, prepared the space, began the project with assistance, and savored the small successes while realizing that revising would continue. Sounds like teaching.

Strategies that work with one student and one set of students can be woefully ineffective with the next. Can teachers take the risk of seeing their school without the borders they find familiar? Successful gardening and teaching require a keen awareness of context. Just as I must study the soil and weather patterns in the former, I study my students and their backgrounds. I read my class or audience. My unquestioned assumptions about gays, Jews, Latinos, or students living in poverty, enter the classroom with me. Our pupils bring their assumptions too, maybe about people like us.

In addition to pedagogical and technological knowledge, if I know the teaching terrain is new to me, or if I'd like to rethink my assumptions, I seek reliable guides. The books we read, movies, programs, and plays we see; the peers we turn to; and the parents— if we teach young children and young adults—can help us be more effective and dare to try new approaches. I'm building my capacities as an educator and building the literacy capacities of my students.

I tell Spanish-speaking families about the Dallas teacher, tears streaming down her face, who described how her father, who didn't speak English, nightly, sat with his children at the kitchen table and asked them to read aloud to him in English. How can we not stop and ache for that dad, for such parents, tired after a long workday yet sitting with their children who read to them in words the parent can't understand. Caring parents are resources. What an act of love, and to think there are schools that consider these parents second class. What a sacrifice for families to let their children go off into another language, a language whose speakers may say, "Don't look back. Our language is a better place."

Thinking of you, I look at my bookshelves. I see writers, my companions, guides, teachers, witty and articulate friends to whom I am a stranger, humans who cared to share their pains, fears, and joys. I again pull out *Lost in Translation* by Eva Hoffman, a book that pierced me to my core when I discovered it. That's what it's like for readers, isn't it, dear teacher? Discovery, the rush I felt years ago, in the dimly lit stacks of the El Paso Public Library when I discovered the entire set of Laura Ingalls Wilder books in the *W*s. I read every one. I still feel the bookjoy many years later.

Hoffman's eloquent memoir took me into a life initially lived in Poland and then transplanted here at the age of thirteen. Holding the book, I'm moved again, asked to remember "how much an absence can hurt." Many students and families know that pain and sadness.

Immigrants, settlers, typical, normal, broken, gifted, disadvantaged, foreign, at risk. To whom do we apply those labels, and who has the power to teach us the labels we adopt? Aren't we all at risk in some way, dear teacher, at risk of not leading the full, rich life that beckons us?

Whether we're talking about doctors, college presidents, or teachers, aren't some viewed as more competent or valuable not for what and how they practice their skills but for their appearance and style, the extent to which they match our image of a respected professional? Do we have a hierarchy among teachers? Might the high school or college English faculty have higher status than those teaching bilingual classes or theories? How do we value one another and learn from one another? How do we build communities of educators that are truly learning communities?

"Who, who, who?" asks the peering and persistent owl, will see the beauty and complexity of each language and culture? Who will treat each young person and family as honored partners in the significant work of education?

Time and quiet allow us to be reflective about our life, what we hope to be in the world and for our own creative work, too. In that silence, we can ponder why we teach what we teach and what we can learn from our fellow teachers and from our students.

We are talented beings. If you want to write or paint more—to be a more inventive teacher or librarian, more open to different kinds of teachers, students, and families who may have different values and customs—what reminders can assist you? Use the little labyrinth I sent to circle into yourself. Guide your students to experience the pleasure of quiet.

"Who, who, who?" asks the owl. Who can do the creative work the world needs from you? No one but you.

Teachers

Like hopeful gardeners,

round the seasons, they plan, work.

Dazzling surprises.

Tips

Invite your students to draw three images: (1) their past, (2) their present, and (3) their future. This exercise can be used at all levels and is also useful for working with families by having parents share their images with their child and vice versa. The exercise is also a helpful means of knowing a colleague better and can be done using concrete, symbolic, or abstract creations.

Create reading spaces in your school possibly with the assistance of students and families.

Exploration for You

Find or draw an object that reminds you of your family when you were the age of your students. If I were I teaching college students, I might draw a car. I was the first in my family to go to college, and I lived at home. My mom would drive me to campus and come back for me until I found friends who would take me home. It seemed so normal and natural for me to be standing under a tree waiting for Mom.

Draw the past, present, and future exercise. Your images may be seeds for writing or further drawing or painting.

Invitation to Write

Write about an incident, happy or troublesome, that involved your parents or family at school. Describe the scene and include how you felt.

Describe a practice that will help you connect more effectively with families.

CHAPTER THREE

Gather Your Materials

Dear Teacher,

"I feel as if someone dumped great building material at my front door," I'd say, "and every morning I have to walk around it because I don't know what to do with it." I was writing my family memoir, *House of Houses,* but didn't hear what I was saying. Not unusual. We begin a project with an idea, almost a dream. I'd sit at my computer and enter family stories that I'd tape-recorded, trusting that the structure of the book would come to me. I smile now at what I didn't hear.

Eventually, I realized I hadn't listened to myself. I did want to build a house—made of words. Family members of various generations would live in the rooms around a central garden and fountain. My word-house was my way of savoring and protecting *cuentos,* stories, and voices that might otherwise disappear, protecting them in print.

Interviewing Mom in her Santa Monica apartment for the memoir, I asked, "Any growing up story you didn't tell us?" Mom laughed her wonderful laugh.

"Did I ever tell you about the May parade?" she asked. The story of her first-grade experience became a scene in the August chapter of *House.* Later, I rewrote the story as a picture book. Although I often read a few scenes from *The Rainbow Tulip* at conferences, I still can become teary at my mother's journey as the first English-speaker in her family, at her boldness and exuberance. Even little ones know that when Estelita, known as Stella at school, chooses all the colors for her May parade tulip costume, she's in trouble.

Mom, the daughter of two quiet Mexican parents who spoke no English, loved to perform and volunteer to be on stage from the time she started school. A widow at eighty-six, she lived her last years at my sister Stella's nursing home. Mom was quick to tell everyone that her beautiful daughter was the boss—well, except when it came to Mom. Although Mom's memory slowly faded, her gracious manner, laugh, beautiful speaking voice, and smile could light any room. Oh, and she was always an incorrigible flirt.

"Have I told you I have a friend, dear?" she'd ask in her eighties.

"A female friend?" I'd respond smiling to myself.

"Oh, no, dear. A male friend. His name is Anthony, Tony, very nice."

Holding hands with Tony didn't keep Mom from warmly introducing herself to any new male resident. My sister called me with romance reports. "*Your* mother!" I was delighted at the news because Mother regularly promised me, "The same will happen to you, dear."

When the nursing home residents practiced for a talent event, "Stand Up and Take a Bow," the star of *The Rainbow Tulip* was ready to join in. Mom didn't remember much about first grade, but the same spirit within her that loved being on the stage—not acting but speaking—lived on.

Although Mom sang when we were little, "Shine Little Glow Worm," and "Daisy, Daisy," a detail my three siblings don't remember, she always said she didn't have a good singing voice. I was amazed, then, that she'd volunteered to lead the group in singing a seniors' version of "A Few of Our Favorite Things." Mom? The day of the big event, Mom, who normally welcomed any opportunity to sit, stood to her full five feet. "Now remember, we *are* senior citizens," she said to the audience, then lead the group in singing,

> Antacids and nose drops and needles for knitting,
> Walkers and handrails and new dental fittings,
> Bundles of magazines tied up in strings,
> These are a few of our favorite things.

Thelma, in her eighties, read original poems, including "Woe Is Me."

> My memory's gone—I don't know where
> I've looked and looked even checked my hair.

Miriam, a professional dancer at eighty-three, did high kicks in high heels. Mom and Tony, both bilingual, sang *"Amapola,"* an old Mexican song about poppies. Whenever they forgot the words, they sang, *"La-la-la-la-la,"* my father's solution when he'd sung.

Ellie, ninety-one, began to teach the *cha-cha,* and because residents were to dance with family members, my sister walked up to Mom. Mom gave her a long look and asked, "And who are *you* going to dance with, dear?" Mom planned to dance with Tony.

In her perfect pronunciation, Mom read some of my poems from *This Big Sky.* She began, as Mom would, saying that each of her four children had special talents. I imagine her in her green pantsuit trimmed with gold holding my book and reading the words clearly and with feeling, ending with bravado, "This sky is big enough for all my dreams."

Years before in El Paso, Mother clapped when my sister Stella performed; now Stella, her namesake daughter, clapped for Mom, the return of the rainbow tulip. The residents enjoyed laughing as their families struggled to keep up with, "If you're proud and you know it, do all three." Laughter and pride deepened community. Families saw that their loved ones belonged, everyone was proud of the performers, and laughter eased the changes each family was experiencing.

The event organizer told the appreciative audience that when she'd asked the cast to think of a special time in their lives, most mentioned their children. She then asked family members to stand and share a memory about their parent. Now that, dear teacher, is when I would have dissolved into a puddle of tears. People would have looked around and whispered, "Where's Pat?" My sister, though, knew she had to begin what would be so difficult for all in the audience. How do we articulate what we feel so deeply?

Stella told about losing her ballet slippers as a high school freshman and being terrified to face an unforgiving teacher. "But I knew Mom could solve any problem," said Stella, "so I asked for her help, and sure enough, Mom found the shoes. Thanks, Mom, for making me feel there was nothing you couldn't do."

I can hear Mom's poised voice, "Thank you, my daughter." My sister whispered, "You were the star, Mom." Mom's eyes gleamed, "That's what I wanted to hear, dear. I loved performing then, and I love performing now." Stella reflected how we were always proud of Mom, and even when Mom had dementia, she still made us proud.

Such stories, this Mom, are part of what I take to any blank page. I bring the voices and sounds from my past: tiny purple flowers of the chinaberry tree, the perfumes my aunt abundantly splashed on at department stores, the time we all spent watering the yard coaxing roses and larkspur to bloom, incense at church; such scents and the complex memories attached to them. I recently heard the food writer Ruth Riechl wisely say, "Death ends a life but not a relationship." Though some family members are now not with me physically, they are always with me.

Are you gathering material about your family, past, and imaginings for your creative endeavors, dear teacher? "You can't go home again," said Thomas Wolfe, but you can, "sort of, when you write about it," writes Margaret Atwood. I like teaching classes on writing family stories or heritage as catalyst for creativity because it's psychologically healthy to be curious about our past, to honor our journey. I once asked workshop students in Minnesota, many of them teachers, to write and illustrate a picture book about themselves or their family. Grumble, grumble. People had their doubts about the project, but they humored me and brought glue, markers, magazines. The books delighted us, and we learned to see each creator in a new way. We were practicing revision. Using mixed-genre approaches—nonfiction, poetry, children's stories—we played with various writing exercises, the play luring us into the deeper family places and spaces.

I read that fabric artist Polly Apfelbaum stacked rolls of multi-colored crepe-paper streamers in a small cardboard box titled, "The Color of My Fate," a response to bride's hope chests. "What color is my fate?" she asked. "All colors, it turns out." I wanted to send this to the editor who, years ago, commented that she liked my story that became *The Rainbow Tulip* but wanted me to remove the part about Mom choosing to be all the colors.

"But it's a true story," I said. "I know," she said (and I quote), "but it's just too pat."

"Facts bring us knowledge, but stories lead to wisdom," writes Dr. Rachel Naomi Remen. I grew up in a bilingual home and have always spoken both English and Spanish. Although I liked writing, there's a lot about myself that I didn't include in my school papers. No one said not to, but I didn't see any examples in books or films or posters of families like mine. How I wish I had some of my work to see what I wrote and thought about, an argument for keeping a journal, of course, so we can look back at whom we were, what mattered, what was troubling or delighting us.

When I began making time for writing, I remembered Mom's cedar or hope chest. Interesting notion and phrase, a box for a bride's hopes. On hot summer days when I was young, I'd occasionally open the chest in my parents' bedroom and look at the romantic cards in which Daddy had scribbled (and I do mean scribbled) his name. I'd gaze at my younger self, a valentine I'd made with my black-and-white picture in the middle. I walked by that chest daily for the first twenty-one years of my life, not really noticing it, as I didn't focus on my Mexican background or the Chihuahua desert in which I'd spent my life. The chest became an important symbol of my adult writing life though, the past as treasure chest, as inheritance. The family I came from, our languages, religion and its beliefs and rituals, our Mexican heritage and its values and customs, memories of family holidays and trips, school memories—all became catalysts for writing.

I paid closer attention to the oft-repeated stories of Lobo, my story-teller aunt, and began asking her questions, taking notes. She handed me wonderful clay that I had the privilege to shape in English and Spanish. I tell bilingual students who hesitate to be proud of their heritage language that monolingual university creative writing students often say they wish they knew at least one other language so that they could braid it into their writing as I do Spanish. Writing, particularly writing poetry, is often about subtle choices, and I have two sets of words to play with, and two literary traditions in addition to what I can grasp of other traditions without speaking the languages. Languages are wealth.

Because little about Mexico was part of my educational experience, I began reading about its plants, crafts, indigenous cultures, folktales, art, myths. I met and married Vern, a professor of archaeology, and teased him that I married him for the facts in his head. He knew so much about Mexico because he studied the Maya. I hadn't then heard the great Agatha Christie quote, "An archaeologist is the best husband a woman can have. The older she gets, the more interested he is in her."

We visited different parts of Mexico just as teachers in Michigan's Upper Peninsula tell me about visiting the countries of their ancestors, Holland and Sweden. Making the journey back helps some of us discover what we'd like to take with us to the future.

In a new way, I savored the desert, its lizards, sand, immense sky, hawks, majestic mountains. The more I noticed, the more I realized the depth of my love for what some perceive as bare. I see the desert's moods and its colors. That's what love does, doesn't it? Makes us attentive. The desert dwells in me. Love of place is powerful.

The dictionary says that the spikenard, an Indian plant, has "fragrant roots." Fragrant roots? What a lovely linking of words. Don't we want all our students and our fellow educators to believe they come from fragrant roots? Don't we want to feel that way? We each have a unique past, a vision for our future, capacities to enrich the world.

What is your beginning place, dear teacher? Spend time reading and jotting down a wild assortment of family memories: songs, celebrations, fights, recipes, teachers. Look at family photos and video or audiotape family members, wonderful aids when you, or someone in the next generation, hears cadences, speech patterns, the phrasings and pauses of family storytellers. Remember Eudora Welty's words, "Long before I wrote stories, I listened for stories." Begin to collect details: family geographies, houses, cultures, characters, images, scents, sounds. Some teachers prepare book bags for students and families. What are you putting in your writing or drawing bag for your future projects—stories, artifacts, photos, even fears? Don't forget your hopes, courage, enthusiasm.

In preparing for a new writing, speaking, or art project, or to pursue an ongoing one, gather your past and imaginings for the journey. For some, that harvest tastes bitter—the violence of colonization, slavery, exile, and discrimination. Grief, like happiness, can be a source, an upwelling of emotions. You may decide that your past or your family's past isn't the clay you want to work. Wouldn't it be dull if writers had a narrow range of options? Whether our gathering becomes possible subject matter or not, there's value in exploring the places, people, music, structures, and stories that are forces in our lives, that are housed inside, the landscape within.

Visiting a childhood house or place, or opening a much-loved children's book, can lead to poems, a painting, a short story, historical research, a scene for a play or a vignette to send the family. Going back, we may not only meet people from other times in our lives but also meet ourselves from other times, gather joy and sadness. It hurts to imagine my father as a boy being physically punished for speaking Spanish at school. Every family knows heartache though at varying levels. Some are memories of feeling like outsiders, because a mom worked at a factory or because a family didn't speak English.

Lucille, a great-grandmother in Oregon, tried so to be a good student during the Depression and hoped her teacher wouldn't visit and see that the wallpaper in her small house was what her mother had—newspaper. In her hands, Lucille hid her sandwich made with homemade bread so the other schoolchildren wouldn't see that Lucille's family couldn't afford the store-bought variety. How's that for ironies?

When have you felt different, that you didn't belong? If one of the motivations for art is to know the self better, our many complex selves, periodically returning to our past seems valuable and healing, a reintroduction. We forget intentionally and unintentionally all that has made us who we are—genetic coding, voices, praise, lonely times. To honor others' stories, we need to honor our own, the journey our family and families made and are making, the landscapes that have housed and shaped us. As Native American writer Leslie Marmon Silko wisely observes, "I will tell you something about stories. They aren't just entertainment. Don't be fooled."

At a San Francisco international conference on women's health, a young woman judge from Africa began her speech with the phrase "I come from a place . . ." I've written various versions for audiences and will probably write more:

I come from a place where the Rio Grande arrives on its journey from the Colorado Rockies. The unsuspecting river became a boundary separating two countries both rich in different ways. I come from a place where many religions are practiced, many languages spoken. The two dominant languages Spanish and English braid and clash, braid and clash. I come from El Paso del Norte, the pass or step to the north, a city protected by a mountain. I come from a place where the sunsets are wealth Wall Street can't comprehend.

When I arrived in Cincinnati in 1989, my first move away from El Paso, a young college student came to interview me. As she removed her coat, she casually said, "I'm American to the bone. My grandmother came from some place in Russia. What are you?" We smile at all she was saying. That search for who we are, our "original self" as Tai-Chi teachers say, seeing ourselves without layers of makeup, without our public persona, is part of our journey.

I joke with my husband that we both dig below the surface. Years ago, someone gave Cissy, my youngest, a long prairie dress and matching brimmed yellow bonnet. Cissy wore it backward, called it her "brain," who knows why. It prompted my poem that ends,

Maybe part of the journey is always backwards,

the careful brushing away of the layers,

personal archaeology, uncovering forgotten,

broken pieces, even in our dreams

until we fit the jagged edges into round wholes

we cherish privately; and occasionally we

break the code, with our fingers read our early

symbols, reunite with the rare spirits we house.

"Cissy in a Bonnet," *Communion*

Wholeness—personal, global. I'm curious about all cultures and feel fortunate when I visit other countries and find myself surrounded by Chinese, French, or Italian. Watching Greek grandmothers, I think of my own. Listening to Balinese mothers, I hear Mexican mothers calling to their children. We are more alike than unlike. In his poem "Eyes," Nobel Prize winning poet Czeslaw Milosz meditates on his eyes when young, and now when they see, "the basic similarity of humans / And their tiny grain of dissimilarity." We are all connected because we share this earth, and we share the journey from birth to death.

This paradox is a challenge in a pluralistic society, realizing how alike we humans are as great literature and other art forms reveal, and yet confronting the necessity to honor our differences and to challenge the systemic obstacles to fully integrating all our voices and talents.

I resisted putting gravel on our labyrinth paths because I like to feel the earth, soil and leaves and wood chips, under my feet. Gardening literally puts me in touch with the earth. Our plantings are about transformation, the garden's and our own.

Children's author Patricia MacLachlan says she always has some prairie soil in her pocket to remind her where she came from. May this imaginary desert sand that I'm pouring into the palm of your hand invite you to ponder where you come from and where you want to go. What will you take with you for your journey as a writer/artist and teacher?

Exploration

Draw an outline of a body, your body. Fill it with symbols (no words) of all you are, of the various facets of you. Let your curiosity carry you along. One of our challenges as writers is how we heed our imaginative impulses rather than allowing our literal, linear, logical judgments, often our daily selves, to squelch those creative possibilities.

Now, in the spirit of heeding those impulses, quickly select a metaphor, a concrete object for your family, one word. Thus, my family is a cactus, my family is a closet, or my family is a piñata. (More on piñatas in my next letter.)

Don't overthink your metaphor but also be wary of too easy or glib an answer. Leap quickly into that crazy idea you were about to suppress. Now on a blank piece of paper, draw it. (Don't worry. My attempts at drawing would make you feel like an accomplished artist. Just jot a quick sketch.) Spend no more than five minutes on the choice and remain loyal to it. Remember: We're practicing how to trust our instincts. Play!

Explore your choice of metaphor. You may respond as you'd like, but if you need some questions, ask yourself, "What appealed to me about the image? Is it funny? Does anything about it frighten me?"

Invitation to Write

Think of your young self. Write the draft of a ten-line poem using this pattern:

Once I _____ ,

but now _____ .

Think of a family member and of a phrase she or he used often. Write that phrase down. Write a paragraph using the phrase repeatedly. Now read what you wrote and edit by removing excess repetitions, maybe using parts of the phrase in spots.

Create an opportunity to work on your autobiography through art. Maybe you and a friend or a group of peers agrees on a meeting schedule. You gather and each write or draw about your life. This can be free-form and timed, or one of you can give a prompt. You then each share what you wrote or drew (or both). And then you share food!

Motivate Students to Gather Their Materials

Dear Teacher,

Piñatas, those delightful, swaying, surprise-filled shapes, raise our spirits, a cheerful way to begin this letter. Marco Polo may have seen decorated or seed-filled clay pots on his travels in China and taken the idea back to Italy. (Clay, a return to our earth symbol). The word "piñata" apparently comes from the Italian, *pignatta,* whose root is from Latin for pinecone. From Italy, the *pignatta* traveled to Spain where it began to be decorated with tissue paper from China. In fact, in Mexico tissue paper is still called *papel de china* (paper from China). I remember being in China and seeing rectangular stacks of colored paper sold for good luck into which intricate designs had been punched. Immediately, I thought of the Mexican popular art form *papel picado,* cut paper glued on string to form colorful and cheerful banners. We see what we think of as traditional Mexican or Latin American crafts like piñatas or *papel picado* and don't realize what a multicultural journey the traditions have made. In many colorful and humorous shapes, piñatas continue to travel to many parts of our world. Like our students, they're receptacles of surprises.

If you're cultivating our first three practices, you're (1) valuing your inventive self and your students' talents; (2) creating quiet time for yourself and your students; and (3) gathering your memories, hopes, songs, and stories. To encourage students to collect *their* ideas and details for their creative work, we can teach strategies for gathering their materials; affirm the worth of the materials; convey our trust that the students have the skills to use their stories, facts, and details effectively; and assure them an interested audience. If their gathering seems like drudgery with little hope of success, how can students bring their most inventive selves to the task?

Some students who dive in thanks to their reading habits, travels, self-confidence, previous writing experiences, and previous writing success will quickly jot down ideas and begin to group and organize them in preparation for beginning their new project. In fact, some students zip through this step too quickly, unaccustomed to thinking and exploring various options. Our challenge, often through the questions we pose, is to help students of varying ages discover the excitement in finding the best options.

Like educators and writers Sonia Nieto, Alma Flor Ada, and Junko Yokota, I have a particular interest in students without strong language skills in English and those wounded by previous negative educational experiences, students who feel anxiety even at the process of deciding what they could write about that wouldn't be "dumb." Their lives can feel dull or embarrassing and their school language sounds flat. That's where you and your wise and inventive teaching step in and aid a struggling writer.

I imagine you exciting them to participate in their own education, to invest in themselves because of your interest, the potential you see. I imagine you reading to and with them, nudging them to read regularly, encouraging them to find books that match their interests, reminding them that reading improves our writing. (I'm continually amazed at college students who want to be published, yet don't read.) You help your students see and hear the connections as readers and listeners between what they read and the ideas (and language) they can generate for their own work. I'm reminded of the Delaware middle school student last year who asked with deep sincerity, "Where do you find the words?" I loved the question. I chatted again about the relationship between reading what others have written and imagining more possibilities for our own writing.

The other memory from the visit is the compassionate teacher who'd secured a school bus to bring students to hear me. She stood up, holding *Doña Flor: A Tall Tale About a Giant Woman with a Great Big Heart* and said, "We love Doña Flor because she's so big, and these students feel so small."

In one sense, it's easy to affirm a student's ideas for writing by quickly saying, "Good job!" How, though, do we really understand the bumpy journey we're asking some students to make from learning to hear and then value their inside voice, and then to dare to present the ideas or stories publicly where their words and stories may look or sound different and may be laughed at? Tough.

"Why do the other kids talk about us that way?" asks a middle school youngster from Mexico. We're in a classroom in Wisconsin thanks to the hard work and determination of the local librarian. The students speak English and are working on their poetry. Some were born in Wisconsin, but their skin color, families, and culture label them outsiders. Sadly, students from Mexico can be treated as outsiders by middle-class Hispanic students in New Mexico, too. This discomfort accompanies students when they prepare to write.

Oh, students can be taught to write dull work by rote and satisfy word counters, but that won't satisfy you, dear teacher. Through your genuine interest, constructive interventions and questions, and your specific praise, you help your students to discover their intrinsic worth and, therefore, the worth of their stories and dreams.

The complexity you face includes that while some students are growing their courage to be able to write and speak their more complex memories and thoughts, others lust to be different and to be rewarded with the group attention that makes shy students cringe. A challenging profession you've chosen.

A few years ago, a Colorado professor handed me a present, a light-green ceramic angel that says *Dream*. She introduced me to her grandson and explained that he'd become excited about books when he heard her read his name "Enrique" in *Tomás and the Library Lady*. Enrique, Tomás' brother, is a minor character in the book, but he wasn't minor to this future reader. The Enrique squirming before me had made a connection and viewed books in a new way. He was important in them. His grandmother was elated, probably in part pleased because she hadn't seen herself in books as a child though she may have been an avid reader. Like many of us, she had found other connections with what she read.

By sharing and discussing books that reflect our students' lives, we validate what they can use for their own writing. We're showing that the names, foods, celebrations, or family rhythms belong in print. After discussing various kinds of stories and text, we offer writing prompts having eased some inhibitions about bringing the specifics of their lives to the classroom. Many creative elementary school teachers assign projects that build on and reveal the knowledge that parents can share with their children. Maybe the parents tell a story they remember or lived and the child provides the illustrations. Inventive educators have families and students draw and write books together, particularly books about the family's life and journeys. Again, to safely share those stories in a class or library, students need to know the stories will be greeted with respect, not ridicule.

A university professor in Ohio paired college students learning Spanish with fifth graders learning English. She gave the children disposable cameras and taught the students about taking (appropriate) family pictures. The children then worked with a college student to write about their families in English using the photographs they'd taken as prompts. Both groups of students learned and produced a wonderful display.

A creative Minnesota teacher worked with her students in learning their family stories. Collaboratively, the students created "think sheets" with questions, then checked out tape recorders and tapes.

When they had the stories and details they needed, they wrote their books that were shared at a family literacy night. This enthusiastic teacher knew that America's story needs the stories of each of our students, that we want them to proudly take their place in the history of this nation, to know and respect their heritage including their literary heritage, and then to choose what they need for their future. She saw the creativity, courage, and tenacity of the families.

One cautionary note. Although students can enjoy sharing stories or poems or paintings about their families and become more of a community in this way, as you know better than I, the concept of family is complex. I wrote *Pablo's Tree* because of my interest in adoption and caution teachers, who often do family tree projects, to remember the complexities of families today. Rigoberto, a very creative teacher and author, had his New York students choose a symbol for sketching their family. Students could choose the standard tree, but they could also select Ferris wheels, tables, rivers, or whatever image conveyed their truth. Sounds like a good exercise for all of us. Family stories can be heartwarming and fill us with optimism, or they can shock us with realities that make us feel helpless, angry, sad.

"This sky is big enough for all my dreams," is a line from my poem "This Big Sky." One of my dreams is that all students will be valued and that in our literature we will hear the songs—the poems and stories—of all our voices.

What are your dreams as a teacher?

Creating a necessary welcoming and respectful community of learners requires an outstanding model (you), skilled teaching, high standards, caring, and enthusiasm. Because you're a leader not only in your classroom but also in your school, I also imagine you prompting discussions with your colleagues about the kind of school you're creating together. "But everything we teach them is undone when they leave the school," teachers in difficult situations say. A wise principal responds, "We must worry about what we can control, the time they're with us. Who knows? Maybe one day our students will influence what's being said or done at home."

Our symbols of seed, labyrinth, and sand apply to our students as writers and artists too. With our support, they perceive themselves as creative beings, they learn to shape or find quiet spaces when necessary, and they learn to gather the many parts of themselves and their past for their writings or drawings. What stories and memories we each carry, sources for writing, speaking, dance, drama, and beginning points for learning history, geography.

The Rainbow Tulip prompted a wonderful story from Jennifer, a university professor who became my friend. Her mother, born in Denver to Swedish immigrants, spoke Swedish until she went to school and married the son of an American ex-patriot and a Mexican woman. The young couple lived in Mexico where Jennifer was born and grew up speaking English and Spanish. She attended the American School but had little in common with the girls from the U.S. When Jennifer came to the U.S. at eighteen, she says that though she looked Swedish, she'd never been there. It was Mexico she missed. Home.

Jennifer describes herself as a "hybrid person" who immediately connected with the mother in *Tulip* because Jennifer also didn't understand the "cultural rituals" at her children's schools. Estelita reminds Jennifer of her own children who were always explaining to her "how things really worked."

Youngsters also delight me with the connections they make. At a memorable school visit in Aurora, Colorado, the day began outside with mariachis and a tree planting ceremony in honor of *Pablo's Tree.* Inside, every classroom door was decorated to illustrate one of my books. A special moment occurred when a fourth-grade teacher told me that when her class was discussing *Tulip,* a student said, "I'm the rainbow tulip in this class! I'm the only Polish boy here." And people wonder why I write books for children. That boy knew what it was like to feel different, but he was in a classroom in which he could openly share what he was.

In contrast, at a workshop for teachers in another state, a teacher cried when she talked about the drawing she'd made about her background, German and Polish. She was surprised by the depth of her feeling, as we were. Her Polish father was ill now, and the teacher so regretted hiding that part of her heritage when she was young and fearful of insults.

Students sense our interest by the way we establish connections with them, in who they are and what matters to them. We're all part of the same family, made of the same clay, our skin and bones. When a student feels your respect, he can take risks, essential for writers. You can create a community, a safe place to gather, write, and explore. Some teachers still perceive their bright Latino or African American students as exceptions, teachers who doubt the power of high expectations and effective support. How do we erase the dangerous foolishness that equates diversity with deficiency, inferiority, low standards, or incompetence? Dr. Alba Ortiz reminds us that having limited English proficiency does not equal having a learning disability.

Let me suggest some resources. First, *ourselves*. As part of an exploration on family and school memories, a teacher in St. Paul drew and wrote that her father wasn't involved in her school life because he'd had limited schooling. One time, though, he helped her with an assignment to make something using only natural objects. The girl and her dad worked together, but because they used shoelaces in their project, the teacher wasn't impressed. "Suddenly, I thought about my students and their parents, how they *feel*. I just couldn't bear to tell Dad that our creation hadn't fared well," she said returning to that feeling of sadness. In connecting with her young life, this teacher connected and understood her students in a new way. The emotional knowledge is within us. It hurts to feel our past or the past a family member endured, but the feeling can teach wisdom, awaken new options and a stronger desire to be imaginative in establishing positive relationships that nurture learning and risk.

Our values also help. Kathy, considered an outstanding teacher by her peers, says, "I try to see the good in everyone. That's how I walk through life. If you really listen, you will hear the good. Students will trust you, and they show you who they are." Isn't that what we all long for, to be really heard?

Our determination is also an asset. Unlike the teacher who asked me, "Do you think my students don't care about learning because they're multicultural?" Sara, who became a librarian at sixty, is full of faith. She arrived at a Kentucky inner-city library and provided programming for students at nearby schools, but she also saw that Latino families moving to the area weren't coming to the library. Although she didn't speak Spanish, she formed partnerships with community members, wrote grants, and established a bilingual story time attended by Spanish and English speakers. As one little girl looked up at the *papel picado* (the rows of cut paper fluttering on the ceiling), heard the group counting bilingually, and helped make *cascarones* (confetti eggs), she said to her mom, "I wish I were Mexican." How often do we hear that? Shouldn't savoring one another's cultures to the point that we want to be briefly part of them seem natural?

Educators like Sara believe we don't have disposable students or families and can't have a functioning democracy without a truly literate, thinking population engaged in making our communities, country, and world safer, more just.

My travels also give me hope. An Asian American principal in Texas goes to the microphone to introduce me, looks out proudly at an auditorium filled with diverse students and begins, "We are rich in cultures at this school." We need a redefinition of what *rich* means, a repeated acknowledgment that economic abundance is but one kind of wealth. We were gathered to talk about writing, united in our shared goal: writing better.

It's challenging but doable, dear teacher, once we remove the filters we've been taught to wear, once we really view our students and families as "created equal," as full of surprises.

We need educational leaders—superintendents, principals, and library directors—with vision, courage, and determination who understand that professional staff diversity is imperative in creating learning institutions that are truly community and national catalysts—rich resources for learning. I can tell when I enter an elementary school if literacy is important to the principal just as I can often tell if children's literacy is important when I visit a library. The principal who begins the academic year by asking her teachers what they read during the summer and who talks about what she read is making a strong statement about the need to remain learners.

Did your teacher preparation programs prepare you for the diverse students we now teach? My heart sinks when I hear a professor tell students that all they need to know to introduce children's literature to the little ones is Mother Goose. We teach what we know, and we see and notice what we've been taught to see. Wise teachers form connections by steadily assessing their students' many levels including their cultural and previous educational experiences.

Writer Luis Rodriguez says he found the words, often credited to him: "It is not enough to prepare our children for the world; we must also prepare the world for our children." Do we—teachers, staff, administrators—apply this concept to our schools? At Hawaii's Bishop Museum, I saw the exhibit "Legacy of Excellence: Highlights of Hawaiian Culture." Do we often enough focus on the excellence, the rich traditions of our students' many cultures, not just the four *F*s—food, fashion, folklore, and festivals—but the discoveries, values, the creative ways a cultural group interacted with its landscape, the broader life view and wisdom of Japan or India? The Hawaiian exhibit included agriculture, water management, music and musical instruments, dance, religious practices, respect for nature and ancestors. We can't force students to be proud, but we can offer educational experiences—texts, video clips, historical context, mini-museums, a rich array of role models—that counter some negative attitudes. Ethnic pride, like faculty diversity, assists students to succeed in schools.

Our memories are encoded in language. Joyce, a professional development presenter, read some pages from *A Library for Juana: The World of Sor Juana Inés,* about Mexico's most famous woman poet, and quickly, she had the participating teachers fold a piece of paper into a literacy memory reminder. (I still have mine.) Teachers wrote a reading memory from their childhood. When the sharing began, a teacher stood and said that at first she wasn't able to write a memory until she realized that the memory of her father stretched out on the floor reading the Sunday comics was a memory she remembered in Spanish, not English. She read the memory translating for those who did not speak Spanish. Can a teacher tell that story to her peers in all our schools and have her experience welcomed?

Imagine the sand I sent in your palm. We share our beautiful, blue planet: the water, air, land. We are interdependent, a notion now celebrated on July 5 as *Inter*dependence Day. Earth, clay, can be shaped into objects of art or whimsy, into the hidden core of piñatas that sway temptingly above us promising surprise.

As we practice gathering our complex selves for our work, we also practice motivating students (and peers) to gather themselves, a learning community, learning to listen with our head and heart. It's a challenge to aim to be a great teacher, but why settle for less?

Tips

Many classrooms enjoy making piñatas. Have elementary students create literary piñatas and fill them with characters, sayings, and artifacts from a favorite book or have them make or draw family piñatas. Such projects are also applicable to literacy celebrations and to teacher preparation programs.

Exploration for You

We are all shaped by what we've been taught. Reflect on your own professional preparation program. If you're a new teacher or librarian, consider writing to that program and sharing your reflections and suggestions. If you're an experienced educator wishing to support your students' creativity, ask yourself what behaviors you've initiated based on new insights or new research on our changing demographics and its implications. If you work in an elementary school, are you consciously involving families as part of your educational work?

Does your family have an immigrant history? If so, how much is known in the family about that generation?

Create an actual, drawn, or written piñata for your family or for your peers and select something special for each family member. This could be a symbol, poem you write, saying, and the like.

Invent a holiday perhaps based on a person or memory. For example, my dear father, Raúl Mora, was born on March 4th, so every year on that date, I send his six grandchildren a reminder to March Forth in some aspect of their lives in his honor, his the generation that sacrificed mightily so that his descendants could enjoy a better life.

Invitation to Write

What is the name of a deceased family member who intrigues you? Write a story or poem in the child voice of that person.

Write a letter to someone you judged based on stereotypes and then realized the error you'd made. Mailing the letter is optional of course.

CHAPTER FOUR

Begin Your Project

Dear Teacher,

"How do you make a poem?" a young student asked. I savored his use of the concrete verb *make*, "poet" from the Greek word *poietes*, maker. When I explored the boy's question, I scribbled notes about what children need when they *make* things like cakes or kites or wooden toys. I deleted that section eventually, but the writing process allowed a far less concrete answer to surface. "One Blue Door" evolved and became part of the collection *This Big Sky*. The poem begins,

> To make a poem
>
> listen: crow calls.
>
> Rain paints a door,
>
> blue in the sky.

I had often walked a wonderful street of old adobes and had seen many blue doors. "Hmm," I'd wondered, "what's on the other side? Probably some interesting little garden." Persistent curiosity, fascination.

Curiosity also prompted me to try "book making," an art form popular with visual artists for designing and perhaps binding books or journals in amazing shapes and sizes. Text is usually optional. Artists design simple or elaborate accordion books, scrolls, and lush books made with beautiful fabrics, special paper, and trimmed with ribbons, threads, feathers, *milagritos*.

Laurie, a sculptor and printmaker who makes such book boxes, albums, pamphlets, and travel journals, occasionally teaches a book-making class she calls "Wisdom in the Hand."

When she invited me to participate, though curious and tempted, I hesitated because I'm always trying to finish writing a book. I decided, though, that the discipline, focusing on hands rather than head, would be good for me. My endless search for grand epiphanies. I know the hand-pleasure of gardening and cooking, working with materials whose familiarity comforts me, of feeling I'm in a space I know well. Because of Laurie, trusting her, I put myself in a psychologically uncomfortable place.

The small group met in her studio—huge windows, bright light, a sanctuary for her spirit I imagine. I'd race across town in the morning and prepare myself for another lesson in patience and humility. The other women had talented hands whether they sewed or made collages. Yup, I was in for another minority experience.

For five mornings, we painted our pages, glued, folded, measured interminably to punch holes correctly. Laurie and my fellow students cut and glued with zippy precision. Mentally measuring and making no mistakes, they'd stride to the paper cutter with the terrifying confidence of an experienced tree trimmer. SLAM! They smiled, executed their tasks with flair. Then there was befuddled Pat.

Next, listening to Bach cello suites, we sewed the binding. That doesn't sound so complicated, does it? The music was to help us experience the rhythmic aspects of the Coptic binding stitch developed in northern Egypt by the monks of the Orthodox church for holding their papyrus pages. Those monks either had a sadistic streak or way too much time on their hands. The process was to be a calming ritual connecting us with generations who patiently and methodically sewed books together. Theoretically, I understood the elaborate patterns that were to discipline the hand, eye, mind, but—I was totally lost. My patient teacher discretely sat by me and helped her challenged student, never letting me fall too far behind. That my two blank books exist at all is thanks to the good humor of the other women and Laurie's patience. She probably needed a glass of wine each time I drove away. My awkwardness reminded me about the mild or not-so-mild anxiety of the unknown. I learned a bit more about myself.

Synergy. I'd written the previous to you and then saw an article about book artists in Cuba, a collective of writers and visual artists that uses recycled and donated materials in their book production. "Wrapped Words," an exhibit of their work, included pages made from sugarcane bark and covers decorated with coffee grounds and birdseed. Do such descriptions and experimentation ideas loosen you up? Visual art does that for me, makes me want to be more inventive.

Seed, labyrinth, sand. If we're steadily affirming our creativity, creating safe places for our explorations, seeking some quiet, and gathering our memories and stories, and—a big *a-n-d*—we have a strong desire to create, we're ready to leap into a new project.

Remember how awkward I felt in my early writing days, the way I felt at the book-making class? I've learned I have to risk discomfort. I trust the process more and move through my fears more quickly, but I can still sigh and wonder, "Will anyone care about what I write?" Painters, dancers, composers, writers, inventors, anyone engaged in creative work is always a beginner. "Beginner's mind," *soshin* in Japanese, is an important habit in Zen practice. Each time I start a poem or project, I begin again. I try not to put pressure on myself. In fact, I'm trying to forget about me, to become absorbed in the verbal clay with which I play.

Writers don't just talk about writing: they write. After years of answering "self-employed" on many forms, recently I thought, "Hmm. I have the wrong boss." That's more of a joke than the truth; I feel lucky to shape many of my days. Goal-oriented, though, and because I love the projects I select, I'm firm about my schedule. Since I enjoy speaking to audiences almost as much as writing, and since speaking helps fund my writing, I travel too much to assign myself a set number of pages per day, but I do try to spend hours writing every week, sometimes on a number of projects. Writers have patterns, practices that yield results. Some, like me, need quiet; others write in coffee shops. I'm sharing my habits not because I think they're The Answer to "How do I develop my creative life?" I share these practices to propose one route until you find your own. Poet Stanley Kunitz reminds us that there are many kinds of artists and many ways to become one.

A planner by nature, I enter my writing goals (in pencil) on my monthly calendar and parts of those goals, on my weekly calendar. I erase and revise my goals often, but the gentle pressure works for me. These appointments with myself are as important as any others. To write seriously, when I'm deep in a book project, I resist answering the phone or even looking at e-mails in the morning. Supportive friends and family understand. It's managing me that's the challenge.

How much time a week or month would you like to, or could you, devote to your creative work? Make appointments for the next month.

I share a new project with very few people to save my creative energy for writing. Once I'm ready to play with an idea, weather permitting—and I'm a weather wimp—I often take a walk. Perhaps the rhythm of walking and the open space free me to enjoy some verbal exploration. I choose a possible poem or story idea and let that anticipation grow. I stroll, receptive to possibilities, active passivity. Some people use dreaming in a similar fashion, think of a project before going to sleep, hope for the subconscious to do its work. My subconscious is just plain lazy and seems to sleep as soundly as I do.

When I first invited writing into my life, I had a row of small cactus in our sunny dinette bay window in El Paso. Sometimes, a pesky, almost invisible spine would lodge itself in my finger. I'd touch the finger repeatedly, trying to dislodge the unwelcome guest that would annoyingly remind me of its presence. That same mild but persistent irritation, the need to attend to something, was what I felt when a story, phrase, or idea demanded attention. I almost enjoyed resisting the idea, letting the desire grow. When I think back to those early writing years, I still see those gold spines. They signaled the incubation taking place within.

I had many more distractions then (three teenagers!), so perhaps that insistence was necessary to bring me back to the page, always a writer's challenge. Although I felt foolish alone at my table wondering why I thought I could write, I tried to be welcoming of my poems, a piece of advice I strongly offer. I'd say to myself, "No one ever has to see this, and remember, you can throw all the first lines away." Intellectually, I knew I could throw the whole thing away, but there was something comforting in the notion that I could just begin to write with no expectation of perfection, wit, or wisdom. I could relax, begin, and discard until perhaps I found some lines or an idea that I wanted to follow.

"You're just the typist," Anne Lamott reminds us. "A good typist listens."

It can be a slow journey to sink inside, to enjoy your interior voice even if it's angry or sad. Emotional memories can be deep places to wander. Courage required. Ideally, every piece we write is an exploration for the writer and reader. Some writers need to know exactly where they're going. Others follow an initial impulse, a scene, a line, a story.

As many writers stress, it's important not to sit staring at a blank page or screen for long. Books advise times for writing, daily writing, generating lists, brainstorming, clustering, or webbing, all helpful strategies for initiating the process. Key word: process. Be open, receptive, and ease into writing or painting your creative project. Your critical self is unwelcome at this phase. Put up a sign: *Critical Pest, Go Away.* Now, I often know before I begin what I plan to work on. If you have no particular idea, go through your journal or idea box. Keep what I call a compost file that includes past pieces you haven't finished, work that you want to work on again, articles or pictures that intrigue you. Your compost will prove valuable as you struggle not only to record an experience for your reader but also to create an experience. Start writing. No one has to see this.

Prompts can be fun. Read a piece you like and push off from it as we do from the side of a pool. Pick a few words to play with or an image or a feeling. I smile at how long it can take me to settle down sometimes, but I'm gently firm and don't buy excuses about needing to wash the dishes or clean out my cabinets. I sit; I write. Some writers prefer to explore writing prompts that veer away from the literal and logical. Many books provide ideas: write about your favorite sound, a grand myth, the color you are at this stage of your life. Drafts are options, paths we're exploring. For years, I had by my computer the Ray Bradbury quote "Don't think," an approach that helped me move along and start writing. "Write about what makes you different," advises Sandra Cisneros.

A welcoming or appealing space or music helps some people; others want a blank wall and no distractions. Few fixed rules in writing except read, write, revise. Each project teaches us. I didn't use music as an aid until I wrote my family memoir, *House of Houses.* Over and over, I played one cassette of Mexican music as I typed. I never turn that music on now. Maybe I wonder if playing it, I'd be nostalgic to be back in the place I spent months creating. I'll soon begin a young adult (YA) version of *House.* Another good excuse to go home again?

Carrying my project with me when I'm not writing can build enthusiasm in my nonwriting time, provided I carry the project lightly. Everything can feel more heightened as I've said that anything could be an idea for the book. I also often read a bit before I sit to write now. I didn't do this early in my writing life, but now, I read work I really like for a while before I begin, like athletes must enjoy and learn from watching pros. Reading poetry by Mary Oliver, for example, I feel language and my love for it welling up. I feel connected to a family of writers that shares my desire to explore and refine with words.

Realistic expectations can ease the discomfort of not knowing where we're going. Resist judging. My first drafts "need plenty work" as the masseuse said about my shoulder. I've even grown rather fond of the "mess" phase, as I have with that phase in cooking or gardening, but that's because I trust the process and know I'll keep my writing appointments.

Do I wonder if I'm deluding myself, if I'm wasting my time? I console myself with the lines from T. S. Eliot.

For us, there is only the trying,

The rest is not our business.

My work is to try. I tell myself that I can't edit what I haven't written. Seldom—if ever—is the final piece all I'd hoped it would be, so I begin another project. I'm practicing, hope I'm improving.

Delight, dear teacher, in creating the habit of writing regularly and in the small successes. Maybe you found the perfect metaphor for what poetry is, or the right voice for a character, or you wrote a very funny line. Enjoy! Just as you would revel seeing your red roses bloom, tasting your cranberry-apple pie, receiving a grant. The pleasure principle is a lure back to the page. Writing, like success, is generative, and creative work generates energy—though not every day. Usually, the more you write, the more writing ideas you'll have. Feel the pleasure you did in finger painting years ago. Relax. Listen. Mess around. Be hope*ful*. We're learning to be better writers, carvers, musicians.

Taking classes can spark ideas and enthusiasm. Recently, Cissy, my artistic daughter who's a mobile cat veterinarian, began a mosaics class. I smiled when she said, "I didn't know how much planning is involved. I was thinking, 'Like, where's the glue?'" Ah, yes. The planning, designing, the dream we're going to create and learn from.

I heard about a college art instructor who urged students to work along, loyal to their projects waiting for a "happy accident." If we can remain receptive, an image or idea or pattern will emerge most days, a tiny seed that if heeded can open from the heat, the intensity, of our interest. Follow. Let the work unfold organically. Surprise yourself, speak kindly to yourself, and support yourself. No negative chatter. And like gardeners, we get to work in comfy clothes. In both endeavors, there's hope of a harvest.

Because revision is perhaps my favorite part of the writing process (sick, isn't it?), I work along, moving steadily, the way I do in my garden, knowing I'll be making changes. I wrote about the similarities between gardening and writing in *House of Houses*. Like a plant, "a poem or story often begins in the dark," deep within us. It "rises, a green, delicate, hopeful song." We're "never in total control, annually surprised by what bursts through."

I tend to begin poetry and children's books writing with a pen on lined, yellow paper. When I'm writing creative nonfiction, I have a conversation with an intelligent and interested person, like you. Writing children's books, I enjoy time with my child self, hoping the sound will be like the sugarcane flute the poet Rumi describes. "The sound it makes / is for everyone." Writing poetry, I imagine Frost's notion of ice on a hot stove. I'm following the poem, tending it. Writing poetry delights me, writing children's books refreshes me, writing nonfiction makes me think hard and refine the ability to link ideas, stories, visions.

Writers on a journey of exploration write the books we need for reasons we may never fully understand. Some write to escape earth's confines, to laugh and make us laugh. I write to learn, discover, connect with people of all ages, to cause readers and listeners to notice those often ignored, to share stories, to relish the pleasure and power of words, to create change, to develop my skills. Irish poet Eaven Boland in her literary memoirs *Object Lessons* eloquently describes her longing to find examples of lives like hers, the lives of other Irish women poets. Those lives, she writes, "would have dignified and revealed mine." We all seek the comfort of images, stories, and lives like ours. "The influence of absences should not be underestimated," writes Boland. I write, in part, to dignify the often unsung lives and experiences of Latinas and Latinos.

Why do you want to spend more time exploring on the page, to experience the zing of writing or painting? My poem to Georgia O'Keeffe about walking with her on my Texas desert ends, "to unfold/giant blooms." Us. We're the blooms. We grow our life, let it develop within, expand, release new energy. Life has its seasons. Write what sustains you. In gardening, I might say, "Prepare the soil, plant the seeds, nurture them." In writing, I suggest a similar approach: prepare, explore, persevere.

If being published interests you, you'll discover how many ideas you'll have when a piece is finally accepted. The challenge is continuing to generate work in a climate of unrelenting rejection. I know. I believe with author Paul Valery, though, that "effort changes us." There's heartache and joy in creative work. So what do you need for the journey? Abundant supplies of faith and hope. Becoming a better writer demands time, effort, and patience. A sense of humor beats spice drops, licorice, caramels, chocolate. Yes, you'll probably need to overcome your dark doubts and make hard choices about your time.

When we believe in the value of making art and that we can be part of the art-making family, and when we believe in the art-making process, we transform our lives.

You can choose your pace, but by choosing to develop your creative talents, you'll make your life richer, for you, your students, and those you care about. After all, you'll have a new dimension of yourself to share. Our life on earth is relatively brief, and our complex, inside selves are worth knowing. We can be so busy meeting the expectations of others and the expectations we've set for ourselves, that we seldom spend time alone, serious time alone, seldom have a true encounter with ourself. We live more attentively when we're writing, savoring life even its pain because we're living more consciously, more deeply. In our more challenging work, we bring a lifetime of thinking, wondering, observing, experimenting, feeling, reading.

Glancing through the books of A. A. Milne's and Beatrix Potter, I'm transported to a world of verbal pleasure, the sweet joy of their language. The world Milne created in which we hear Winnie the Pooh makes my wee heart expand. I smile in and out, feel my three children sitting next to me years ago in their soft pajamas when we lapped up the language like Winnie lapped up the honey. In Milne's poetry collection, *When We Were Very Young*, "The Alchemist" sits in his room in his "big wide-awake" hat and writes. The task he repeatedly pursues is struggling to create magic.

Santa Fe artist Maria Hesch painted her bit of magic. Inspired by the style of Grandma Moses, Maria painted her Northern New Mexico heritage. Both women were self-taught. In her own words, at a certain age, Maria "got the nerve to start." How happy I was to discover her work and then use it for *Maria Paints the Hills*.

So let's regularly don our "big wide-awake" hat and create. You'll hear yourself, frustrate yourself, but nourish yourself. "If I knew all I should," wrote the Mexican poet Sor Juana Inés de la Cruz, "I would not write." Dear teacher, our stories and poems are not complete without yours. Practice exploring your creative talents. What's my process? I'm a reader, I set goals, I'm firm about my writing appointments with myself, I banish negative comments, I persist.

When asked what animal I'd like to be, I choose a bird, probably a dove. Such vulnerable creatures, but I think of the rush of flight, the faith in wings and winds. What amazing views doves enjoy, they visit companionably, and they voice their pleasure. What about you, what would you be? My friend Gie once said feathers are messages. Imaginary Gift 4, I send you a feather, a message wishing us the faith to let go of the familiar.

Exploration

Select an object that reveals what you value. Explore its symbolism for you through some aesthetic response, such as writing, painting, composing.

Experiment with physically making a book either by following simple rules for folding a piece of paper or by trying something more complex.

How much time this week and this month did you say you would devote to your creative project? Write those appointments in your calendar—and keep them.

Invitation to Write

Describe your home or a favorite space from the perspective of an animal you would choose to be.

Complete the following sentence with a noun:

Writing (or knitting, etc.) is _____.

I might say, for me, writing is green, for example.

Expand your metaphor in prose or poetry.

If you like the book you made, write in it, or perhaps, team with a partner and either explore both forms—the making and writing, together—or combine your skills.

Assist Students to Begin Their Projects

Dear Teacher,

I've been thinking of my home city of El Paso and the bookjoy of the library summer reading clubs. Did you belong? I was happy with a certificate, but now kids receive incentives such as T-shirts and pizza coupons. Summer book clubs today are planned for teens and adult readers, too. I always urge students to join the club and continue developing their reading skills. Experiencing the pleasure of reading all kinds of books in such clubs was one of the catalysts for founding the family literacy initiative now known as "Día," El día de los niños/El día de los libros, Children's Day/Book Day. Día is a great kick-off to summer reading promotion. More about Día in a future letter.

In elementary school and part of high school, I believed my teachers were all knowing. Surely, there wasn't a grammatical question that Mrs. Morton couldn't answer, a Latin passage that Sister Charles Johanna couldn't translate, a poem Sister Godfrey and her wild gray eyebrows didn't understand. They were my heroines, their minds and eyes sparkling with knowledge. I longed to be one of them, to stand in front of my obedient students.

I wish I'd been writing when I started teaching, both for the personal benefits and because I would have been a far-better teacher. I could have talked about the structure and music of language, but from concrete experience, from my questions and wrestlings.

What have you discovered about the art of teaching? What have you discovered about assisting students to float rather than thrash in the writing process, the poet William Stafford's inviting metaphor? As we practice to become better writers, we can share what we're learning with our students, how we continue when we're discouraged, how we revel when the words fit together. The *zing* of writing.

Part of the context for our work, unfortunately, is that because commercialism needs consumers, billions are spent convincing us that shopping is hip, sophisticated, nostalgic, fun, essential—whether buying tickets to a race, the lottery, the newest car or gadget. Shopping is our right and reward, a smidgen of heaven on earth. The life of the mind? Pondering a challenging book or struggling to describe that pink sky in our own unique way? Not much profit to be made there. But if *we're* excited about what we're reading and writing, our enthusiasm and discoveries can lure our students, *some* of our students, to explore too.

Students need to see us practicing what we urge them to do. Middle school teacher and writer Nancy Atwell's willingness and enthusiasm for reading and writing with her students, and elementary teacher and writer Katie Wood Ray's mini-lessons on craft issues in writing are instructive examples. Just as students profit from a math or science teacher's explanation of how she solved a problem, students profit when you share how you prepare, explore, and persevere. A fellow writer, you can concretely talk about your strategies for beginning a piece or resources for unusual information. How do you deal with your frustrating moments? Students, then, can share their approach in a community of writers, a community supporting one another in the difficult process of clear and evocative expression. It's a tall order and, like most things, can seem easy until we try. I tell students that everyone in the room is a writer—students, teachers, the principal or professor—and that we all secretly want to be better writers. I know I do. Every day I hope to be a better writer than I was yesterday.

Students of all ages can arrive at our classrooms as reluctant writers. This isn't usually true of the little ones who early on ideally encounter support, enthusiasm, and clear directions. They plunge in. Ask them to select the animal they'd like to be and to inhabit it and write a story in the voice of that creature, and they're ready, excited. And they often like what they've written. That willingness to take imaginative risks sadly diminishes as students move through our educational system. We humans wisely learn to protect ourselves. We repress our initial, perhaps wild and crazy ideas, for fear of being laughed at or perceived as different, weird. Young students can be exuberant about their ideas if their sincere responses are incorporated respectfully into the learning. They haven't created elaborate filters for their imaginations and haven't experienced repeated failure.

Often, by the time students reach college, their apprehension shows. My friend John, a writer and professor who prepares students to teach writing, says, "My students bring me their heavy hearts, their memories of failure. I have to help them unlearn their fear of writing." He also wisely adds, that because we never know "who might do something genuine or even marvelous, all need encouragement."

Many fine programs have been developed using a writing workshop model to counter previous narrow and prescriptive writing experiences and to provide techniques and procedures that foster creativity while teaching conventions. Reading and writing are such essential skills, especially in a democracy, essential for civic participation, for being a lifelong learner, for economic opportunity, and for the full development of the person. Language and languages liberate us to explore and defend our beliefs, to articulate our individuality, to sing our song in this world, however gravelly our voice may be.

I'm excited about my projects because I choose them. Although we must prepare students for writing tests and hurdles, allowing students to also choose topics or styles is necessary to spark their imaginations. I encourage students to write about their interests, strengths, dreams, inventions, what matters to them, or what they want to learn about. If they aren't actively engaged in their writing, they neither learn nor produce work to share. Wise and experienced researcher and writer Lucy McCormick Calkins reminds us that children need to write "about what is alive and vital and real for them." All of us need that. To persevere, beginning writers also need to believe that communication is important and rewarding, that someone cares about them and about what they say. Looking at a blank page, they need to feel what we need, that initially, they can safely take risks. To pass the writing tests, students need strong preparation. I ache remembering the panic, fear of failure in the eyes of Texas fourth graders who dreaded their upcoming examinations.

Working with families who may not understand the importance of their support in developing their child's writing skill can be crucial. Children learn to swim and ride a bike both because they don't want to avoid embarrassment and because they are often cheered to victory. Who cheers for the struggling writer? She also needs to experience occasional success. We can coach parents. Also, regularly rewarding success through having students comment on what they liked best in a paper or painting and occasionally marking only what you like in a student's work, finding and articulating his strengths, also helps him to take risks as can collaborative writing. We all need sincere and specific praise.

Are your fellow educators who teach writing also writing themselves? What a difference it makes when I meet students whose teacher is exhilarated about language and writing. A young, red-headed student at an Albuquerque bookstore told me how much she loved to read and write. A prolific writer, she was receiving plenty of support at home and school. Burbling on about her writing, she said, "I have to read one of my poems sitting down because it always makes me so dizzy." She'd tasted the power of language! We want all of our young students to grow into their own green song, don't we?

Students can be so intense when they're taking writing seriously. I think of a tiny boy in the back of an auditorium who stood and asked in a very serious voice, "What is your writing process, and do you web?" In New Jersey, a group of private-school third graders with Bev, a gifted teacher, took great pride in showing me the poetry memo pads they carried to jot down ideas for their poems. Bev knew that although there was little ethnic diversity in her class, diversity in learning styles and backgrounds existed, but she had no doubt that each student was a poet, and neither did they. Did they write better than they would have had they lifted their pencils with heavy doubts? They had been taught to work at their craft and to enjoy their successes and, thus, were freer, swimming happily in language.

With adults, I savor watching a group experience the work of poets who inspire me and them. I often begin my writing workshops the way I begin my own writing time except that my reading at home is silent. We begin the workshop by reading aloud. Sometimes, either a student or I will read a piece we like. We don't discuss the selection. We're just settling into language that sings, letting it transport us further into ourselves in a welcoming quiet. We're all writers listening to ourselves until we're tempted to explore on the page. We're listening for a seed to a song.

This kind of writing experience that can also include music is completely different from timed writing, a skill students also need. For students not to experience the necessity of quiet and mulling as a prelude to their imaginative work, though, is to deprive them of the experience that you and I as writers know is essential. Writing is exploration. The patience to be still and to listen within is learned.

We model the connection between reading and writing by reading a variety of wonderful books or selections aloud to our students and model the connection between quiet and writing by having a few minutes of silence as preparation. Some teachers use music to help students sink into a more meditative state. We use the strategies we're trying on ourselves, acknowledging the struggle in a "just do it" world to also stop and listen. Selecting what to read to help prime the pump for students requires that we know them and that we respect their better interests. Part of preparing to write can include drawing first or doodling and noodling time. My receptivity is not the passivity of watching a TV or movie screen, zoning out. I'm relaxed but alert like someone fishing. I'm waiting for a tug on the line.

Can we resist trying to make our students sound like us and assist them to develop their own unique voices, at times incorporating whatever languages enrich their home lives? It's such a difficult balance, insuring that our students develop the necessary skills to communicate effectively in English applying necessary conventions and yet honoring their voice and creating opportunities for language-play free of our red or green scolding pens.

I didn't learn this until I began to write. Some of what I write about most, being of Mexican descent, never appeared on my successful English papers. No teacher ever encouraged me to listen to myself and to create the silence to hear my voice, until Andrea Otañez, the editor of my essay collection, *Nepantla: Essays from the Land in the Middle,* called me on the phone after reading a section and said the beautiful words, "Tell me more. I want to hear more from you on this."

I was in Cincinnati, and I still remember the energy with which I began to type. I was alone and giddy. Someone really wanted to know what I thought and felt. What a gift, the gift we can give our students and which I so wish I'd known to give years ago. Though teens may conceal it, students of all ages are thirsty for our interest and approval. When a friend's son, not a stellar student, told his mom his SAT scores, he asked, "Are you proud of me, Mom?" It's hard to remember that vulnerability when we work with groups of teens wearing their protective armor. I recently finished *Dizzy in Your Eyes,* a book of love poems for them, such pleasure, the opportunity to spend months listening to their internal voices.

Maria, a librarian in Florida, knows the impact teachers have on tweens and teens. Born in Puerto Rico, she left the corporate world to become a librarian, to positively affect middle school students. She credits her eighth-grade teacher with "making all the difference. Even though I was shorter," Maria says, "she didn't talk down to me. She seemed to know all the quirkiness of teenagers." Maria came from a very strict family in which even to talk to a teacher could have been viewed as a sign of disrespect, but this teacher built a bridge of interest, and Maria is still in touch with her and still inspired by her. What an impact educators have.

I watch Alfredo work with middle school students, moving around the room as groups discuss and think together. He's steadily affirming, and through insightful questions, he's expanding his students' perspectives.

Teachers at an institute in Chicago likewise mentioned the connection of their past to their profession. "I became a bilingual education teacher because I went to a school where I was made to feel ashamed of speaking another language." In contrast, a woman who grew up in Patterson, NJ, said, "I became a teacher because I had great teachers." These teachers knew that students "draw from our energy." "Teaching children is my gift," said an inspiring woman.

When I speak to preservice teachers, many excited about their chosen career, I encourage them to protect that enthusiasm in spite of all the paperwork, time frustrations and, perhaps even more, from any apathy or negativity within the faculty. Educators can give up: on their students, their colleagues, administrators, themselves. Luckily, many remain engaged because they may love what they teach, love their work, or because they're fascinated by their students. Like parents, some educators may be tempted to pull out great chunks of their hair at times, but they find satisfaction at all three levels.

We assist students to discover that they can indeed improve their writing just as they can improve what they've drawn. We help them understand the need, in Donald Murray's words, for an "insulated chunk of time" for our drafts. We teach them the revision skills we're practicing: to settle into ourselves, to start doodling or sketching while mulling if that helps, to brainstorm and connect ideas, to move along positively knowing that we'll have a chance to revise, to let ourselves relax and fly a bit. When we believe in our students and connect with them, when we're alert not to ask them to leave part of their core at home, we assist them to succeed. You and I can often see through the bravado with which some students protect themselves. No student logically wants to fail.

Practice is also needed in strengthening our connections to families when we work with younger students, sharing the writing process and theory with parents in their own language if necessary. We can inventively negotiate language intimidation when we emulate Piglet. "Piglet was so excited at the idea of being useful that he forgot to be frightened anymore." The relationships we establish with parents who don't speak English or don't have a literacy legacy may strengthen a family, provide flights of fancy as well as practical information through books. I remember a color photo of five Afghan women in the newspaper a few years ago. Of varying ages, they were sitting on the floor, heads covered. Their curious faces peered at the books in their hands. The headline said, "Long in Dark, Afghan Women Say to Read Is Finally to See."

By expending energy, we teach ourselves that change requires effort. We teach ourselves about our capacity to work, to influence other lives but also to influence our own. We have the opportunity to create writing pathways or barriers for ourselves, our students, their families, our peers. Is your school climate supportive of the artistic work of staff, teachers, administrators? It's so easy to define professionalism in narrow ways and mentally to put those around us in narrow boxes. Cynicism squelches creativity.

Because change is slow, maybe a faculty group begins slowly. In a book-making group in Santa Fe, members pair up with someone they'd like to know better. Would your peers or a group within the faculty want to try this? You could, for example, choose a partner, and after agreeing on some joint goals—possibly supporting one another in your creative art and creative teaching—agree to exchange postcards, or write brief illustrated letters that could even become a book, or get together and design a collage about the creative work you're doing or about your sources of inspiration. Nothing that takes a huge amount of time but connecting in creative ways. Your partner becomes the occasion for releasing your creative selves.

Maybe you reach out, the English teacher and the ESL teacher, the math teacher and the art teacher, unsatisfied by the distances that keep you from working together for the young who need us and from learning from one another and supporting one another. Perhaps the faculty decides to have fun and create a mural. Maybe, you also decide to create text for the mural. When we create, we discover that inventive part in each of us. The educational circle begins to make more sense.

Seed, labyrinth, earth, feather. The feather, once a writing tool, is a symbol of flight, ascendance that's important for us in our writing and in our teaching. We can boldly exceed our expectations in both. Our students need our faith to soar aided by our experience and support, to explore the pleasure and power of language(s).

Tips

Share an object with your students that's important to you, and ask students to bring one that's important to them. Use the objects as writing prompts. I've sometimes let students lay their objects out and then had a writing activity before students tell about their treasure. The treasures of others can provide interesting topics for our own writing.

Students of all ages can enjoy calligrams, shape poems, images made of words, a poem about a frog, for example, written in the shape of a frog.

Exploration for You

Sharing your own work with your students can be a fine source of inspiration for them. Might you want to read them your animal poem or whatever seems appropriate and then ask them to use that as a model and try a piece of their own?

If you work with younger students, you can invite students and their families to write and illustrate books together. You might select a theme such as journeys or memories.

Invitation to Write

A few years ago, I was asked by the Children's Book Council to write an essay on a book or books that were important to me as a child. What an enjoyable project! I wrote about the Childcraft series and what delight I found in the orange covers of those books, particularly the poetry volume.

Think back to your young reading self, if you were a reader, and write about the books that gave you bookjoy. If you weren't a reader, write about how you felt about that. What books did you try, and what were your reactions?

My friend Cathy, a school librarian in Phoenix, says she invites authors to visit because she's creating good memories for her students. Write about three of your strategies for creating good memories for your students.

CHAPTER FIVE

Revise

D ear Teacher,

Plane flights allow me to practice quiet, to let my imagination fly along with the plane. I've always enjoyed looking for forms in clouds and these last years have looked for figures in the flames of our kiva fireplace. En route to El Paso some years ago, I discovered a new shapes game. Gazing down on the Chihuahua desert, I began discovering shapes on the landscape. It was great, private fun to spy sights amazing as the Olmec colossal heads from Veracruz. I saw imaginary prehistoric creatures like an elongated giraffe with six legs; and a skinny, skinny male figure resembling the work of one of my favorite sculptors, Giacometti. The landscape invites my attention.

I enjoyed the comments of Easterners on the flight who were mildly and not so mildly horrified at the absence of trees. "It's so— beige. Does it ever rain?" a young woman asked peering down as the plane was landing. Having spent years in the glory of Midwest maples and oaks, I understood the young woman's surprise. Like the blank page, though, the desert can become a magnet. Both offer many gifts.

A risk for any of us in returning to the city we called home is how *other* people have gotten older. I scurried to visit my aunt and uncle, then in their eighties, theirs perhaps the last house where family of the previous generation welcomes me, and where I'm the youngest in the room, the niece they've known since birth. Aunt Carmen, a wonderful cook, gardener, seamstress, and painter, was struggling with aphasia caused by a stroke. Ever determined, she had spruced up her garden and prepared a good lunch complete with marble cake. Once an active and vibrant woman, now she smiled and listened, unable to control her words though her memory and mind remained keen. I ached watching how humans accommodate to unwelcome change with grace.

"Have you been telling yourself any stories, Unks?" I asked. When I'd interviewed Uncle Lalo for *House of Houses,* I'd discovered that the uncle I thought I knew had a secret life. Years ago driving alone the long miles along the border for his work with the U.S. Boundary Commission, he'd developed the habit of telling himself stories to stay awake, stories that he kept perfecting. He chuckled, almost embarrassed at the habit.

"You're going to think I'm crazy," he said, "but something will happen that triggers an idea, and then I just start developing the story, you know, to entertain myself. I use names or stories from my past, details about me or my family and friends, but I add them to the story, working it out until it's just right. Usually they're set in the West." He began telling me the current story, savoring every detail. At tender scenes, he teared up. The private lives of those around us. My fit uncle, who had always exercised, said that in the evenings while my aunt watched television, he'd circle the inside of the house for forty-five minutes, working on his stories as he walked, revising.

Remembering this visit, I smile thinking of the practices I've been suggesting:

> Practice 1: Deep inside, he valued his creative self and took pleasure in what he created (and with no outside validation such as publication).
> Practice 2: He knew the importance of quiet.
> Practice 3: He gathered the details of his life and his imagination.
> Practice 4: He regularly explored a new project, in his case, a story.
> Practice 5: He revised his story and regularly repeated the first four practices, part of the circular journey, in his case, literally, as he walked around the rooms of his home.

Each practice poses challenges. Which is hardest for you? Although I've learned to value my creative self and practice habits to affirm that, it can be a challenge when the rejections exceed acceptances. I tell my children that "rejection" is my middle name. I spend quite a bit of time alone now, so I have the advantage of solitude not available earlier in my life. (I wouldn't trade those mothering years for anything, of course.) Gathering our complexity and bringing it to the page or canvas requires challenging the self to go more deeply into the work, to risk experimentation. When Picasso, certainly an artist most of us associate with inventiveness and breadth, was struggling to capture emotion in painting, he hung images by El Greco around his bedroom. Such a detail is comforting, isn't it? We struggle to improve; we learn from one another and from within.

I think our friendship can withstand the repetition of the statement: I revel in revision. I know: it's an acquired taste. Einstein was reported to say, "I will a little think," when pondering a problem. Don't be discouraged if you're not initially drawn to the task. It's through practice that we develop that mulling and tweaking habit. Students of all ages groan audibly, and friends look at me as if I've admitted an embarrassing vice, like chewing tobacco. 'Tis the truth though. Taking my text and tightening it, moving sections, replacing words, weaving sounds together, listening to language play, listening for a certain tone or pitch, gives me a linguistic high. Oops. Another minority moment I fear. I like Annie Dillard's metaphor of tapping the lines we write with a hammer. (That was "tapping" not smashing, and it's a very little hammer.) After years of attention, writes Dillard, "you know what to listen for."

It's understandable and probably important that beginning writers at any age fall in love with their work. Many would not continue without that emotional satisfaction. Like all romances, though, a bit of objectivity is eventually helpful. Some writers, like dancers, decide to add a more complex step to the process. Someone can enjoy dancing for the pure fun of it, and one day decides, "I want to improve certain moves, to learn some new steps, to challenge my feet and body."

"It is only by selection, by elimination, by emphasis that we get to the real meaning of things," wrote fellow desert lover Georgia O'Keeffe. Revision is the part of the writing process that invites us to read and reread our work, to delete, clarify, add a story or example, to burrow into what we're exploring and discovering. I'm not referring merely to verbal complexity, to linguistic pyrotechnics.

The older I grow

The blacker I do be.

What clear lines by poet Lucille Clifton. We don't know how many drafts it takes a writer to amaze us with her compression. What opportunities for pondering, discussing, writing. As we age, what do we "be" more? We can toss out flip answers: more gray, more forgetful, more creaky, but what about the deep stuff, what am I *more* as I age? You and I could have a long lunch on that topic. To write that deeply requires courage, but what a gift she gave me. I've quoted her words for years.

Certainly, I get frustrated and discouraged that I seldom meet my self-imposed deadlines because it takes me more time than I ever anticipate to revise. As I read and reread, I'm not only changing words or moving text, I'm listening, thinking, discovering. These solitary ruminations and experimentations that can transform a line or paragraph are the zing of writing. It's the pleasure of performing a complex task with my whole being to the very best of my ability and hoping it will bring others pleasure or insights. I'm like the gardener who works on a flowerbed and moves, adds, and removes plants, studies her creation, makes more changes, reads more books, brings all she knows about gardening to the task, and then finally, stands back, enjoys cool water, and says, "Oh, I think it works," savoring the thought of others enjoying the aesthetic experience.

Poet Stanley Kunitz wrote that a gardener is "helping to create a living poem." I remember a woman in Greece whose garden I admired. I'd watch her watering and "revising." When I discovered that she spoke English, I told her how much I liked her creation. "It's my present to all who walk by," she said.

For years, I've saved an article about a family known for making the delicious, expensive cheese, Parmigiano-Reggiano. A young man in the family commented that apprentices begin in their teens. "What they cultivate then," he said, "—and what they continue to refine— are solid instincts for milk." Isn't that a splendid notion? Based on our experiences and interests, sometimes passions, we seek to develop a "feel" for the material we work. The romantic story begins with luck, as such stories usually do, the chance meeting, having the opportunity to get to know and study clay, tiles, wood, watercolor, words, milk. The love can be at first sight or a gradual deepening of the attraction. The entanglement becomes irresistible, painful, absorbing, glorious. We notice the details and listen for clues.

Ironically, though we teach students a necessary and keen awareness of audience—an important skill they'll need to know to effectively articulate their beliefs about a school bond issue, complaints to their landlord or humorous stories at presentations for peers—you and I sometimes need to forget about audience in our deeper work. If I'm busy worrying about what Latinos or women or family or Catholics or conservatives will say—I'll never write, or never fully write what I could. With trust and hope, we leap into language or languages and bring our funny, sad, curious, and angry selves to the page.

We struggle to be attentive, to hear way below the surface, the ideas like water quietly flowing along. We rethink what we've written. Like experienced hands revisioning the clay of an initial creation, we explore. Some writers are just plain unromantic and, like many students, want to write a piece once and move on. The more subtle relationship with language bores them. I love the long relationships, engaging with text.

That milk image lingers, maybe because I'm a cheese-lover. How do we develop a feel for words, and how do we continue to refine that skill, that intense listening? Susan Brind Morrow, author of *The Names of Things,* serves as a guide. She writes, "Language is fossil poetry." Can we think of words that concretely and study them with that kind of curious attention? Can we listen to words talking to one another as poet Mary Oliver suggests?

Careful reading is a habit that prepares us both for writing drafts and for revision. The "feel" for language that we desire helps us hear the flat and flabby phrases or paragraphs. I've joked that my favorite key on a computer is *backspace.* Revision is the opportunity to exceed and surprise myself, to be so busy listening to a paragraph that I surrender control when that's needed. I work as long as my time and energy allow on a first draft and then set the piece aside, preferably for at least a day. Sometimes, I can't resist beginning to change words or forms. The best phase has begun!

I then begin to read the draft with more attention. What are the opportunities for shaping this text? What is it really about? What is its undersong? Am I settling for the predictable? Again, no one needs to ever see this phase. I'm experimenting. I'm noticing what ceramicist Robert Turner calls the "revolving sense of reconnections between things." I'm noticing the threads and like an industrious spider, spinning. Turner talks about how we're affected by what we make, and how we need to resist control and allow chance to enter, to feel that movement between faith and action.

I'm mulling but at a deeper level in revision. I'm pondering the project, assessing whether the words are a river carrying the reader along without lulling the reader into a sweet slumber. I'm open to possibilities whether from my critical side that nudges me to move text or from the part of me that has been incubating ideas that appeal to me. I'm alert to keep the seeds of desire alive and allow them to soften, open, flower.

A mumbler, I sometimes read a piece aloud, particularly poems and children's books, as an aid to improving them. Revision is more complex than editing, that final polishing that is important but not nearly as exciting.

To write more regularly and write what excites and sustains you, deepens your commitment to the habit, writing groups can help. Do you belong to one? Enjoying a community of writers composed of friends or peers provides helpful support for your work and for your work with students. Time is such an issue for all of us, but if you want to improve your writing, consider joining or forming a group. You may want to get to know your colleagues better and form a peer group, or you may want to keep your school/campus and writing life separate. The group could meet monthly and be a reading and writing group or focus on the writing later. Settle for nothing less than a supportive group. Trust is essential. Writing is risky enough for some people without having a mad ego attacking your work.

I was a university administrator raising three teenagers when I first started writing with focus and didn't have the time for a group then. When I moved to Cincinnati and began devoting more time to writing, I started a group that became a wonderful help. I purposely selected writers I liked as people but whose styles weren't necessarily like mine. We learn from difference. Murray, Norma, John, and I met once a month in one another's homes. We'd visit for a few minutes and then share our poems. Afterward, we continued chatting over dessert.

Groups force us to think about writing and to produce new work. They provide a place to share the titles of helpful books and to plot how to organize our life so that we can read and write more. Our group never arrived without a new poem although sometimes the pages were fresh from the printer. We took turns reading our poems aloud before anyone saw the words, and then we listened to someone else read our lines. We were friends focusing on the poem, listening intently. When we discussed a poem, thinking of how to strengthen it, the author never argued. She or he listened to the comments and suggestions and took notes in self-interest. When we were finished talking about the poem, the author could ask questions. Notice that no time was spent by the author defending the writing.

Our group made us better writers; the support helped us persevere. My three friends, authors I respect, were also working on *their* writing, experiencing frustration and elation. Our writing community lightened our load in this world. We laughed lots, savored friendship, and shared concern for one another's work sweeter than all the very nondietetic mint chocolate chip ice cream we enjoyed.

Forming a group that's fun, energetic, honest, and respectful requires planning. I had the good fortune to be in a workshop with the poet Sharon Olds and have used some of her approaches with groups I've led through the years. Small groups may not require the following admonition; larger groups almost always do. Everyone, the quiet and the highly verbal, needs to accept responsibility for being a good self-monitor. "Airtime" is limited, and it's unfair for someone to speak too much no matter how bright, funny, or clever she is, and unfair for some not to speak at all. Balanced participation is the goal.

I stop a workshop halfway through a session and ask each person to silently ask himself if he has shared enough, has used his time and can now practice listening, or if he has not shared enough and needs to nudge himself for the benefit of the group. A writing community can encourage innovation because we gather not to judge or compete, but to experiment and explore, to take writing risks together that we might not take alone, and to support one another in those risks.

When I first started writing, I thought about folk artists as my models perhaps because I grew up on the U.S.-Mexico border and enjoyed the market in Juárez. Clay frogs and snakes, wood fruits, and whistles all delight me as does watching folk artists at work. They seem to find quiet joy in their craft and often have a sense of humor, a twinkle in their eye, as they sit long hours listening while they whittle or shape clay, in the world—yet in their own world. Steadily, they work to extend a tradition and often to introduce their own innovations without the trappings of glamor and attention that can indeed be traps. Slowly, they polish their work. Imagine a master woodcarver, working a piece until it almost glows from within, a bit of the maker shining inside, the goal of revision, refreshing as cool water after hard labor.

In the desert, we know water's importance. My husband studies the ancient Maya and how civilizations managed their landscape and harvested water. Because of the seasonal rainfall in the Maya wet/dry forest, Vern believes they sculpted the landscape to create reservoirs on hilltops, thus ingeniously creating sources of water for the dry spells. You know where the analogy is going.

The practice of revision can include dry spells. What are the reservoirs to which you retreat to remain buoyant, to fuel your creative work? Where are your oases, not the mirages, but the oases you create, be they in your home, your weekly routine, or your year? Sometimes I need the laughter, stories, and intimacy of family, and sometimes I need quiet for reflection. When we're dragging our heavy selves to continue with our work—particularly revision, which seldom yields quick rewards—our rhythms need to include times of intense focus and times to refresh our parched selves.

We need to know our interior landscape, to sculpt the landscape of our lives to create sources of energy and creativity, aware that we will become depleted as writers, teachers, and leaders and need to know what and where our reservoirs are, to restore our spirits to their healthy selves. "Cuentista," storyteller, the final poem in *Agua Santa: Holy Water* ends,

> In any desert, she can bow her head
>
> and sip from her own arms.

Robert Frost's poem "Directive" ends with the wonderful notion of offering us a children's goblet he has hidden. He ends, "Here are your waters . . . / Drink and be whole again." Drink. We cannot persist in our work without refreshment. I send you water in a child's goblet.

Versatile in form, water is also a versatile symbol of both lightness and the dark depths of the subconscious. We can experience physical thirst, but those of us who love words also thirst for the river of language, streams of languages (human inventiveness) form *un río grande*. This large river soothes us, its playfulness delights us, its rage can trouble or frighten us. And like a river, language can be politically constricted to become a border. Free, the river of language quenches our deep human thirst for communion and community.

Rhythmic river, rhythmic creatures. With no effort of our conscious will, our eyes blink, blink. In our various skins, our hearts beat, thump, thump; within us, a river flows. Far apart, we still breathe together. And together we thirst to live significant lives.

Exploration

Draw your reservoirs. Do you turn to them wisely in your life, or do you allow yourself to become too depleted? If the latter, why and how might you begin to change this pattern?

List three of the hardest things you've ever done in your life. What were the resources, internal or external, that assisted you to persist and succeed? Are those experiences relevant to creating a writing or painting goal for the coming year?

Invitation to Write

Select a word, cherished or new. Hold it in your hand as you would hold a fossil. Study it. Turn it over. Smell it. Taste it. If so inclined, discover its history or create your own. What is its connection to poetry? Write about this word as fossil poetry. Write a poem about the word, to the word, or a poem inspired by the word.

Invent a word, as I invented *bookjoy*. Let your mind mull for a few days.

Have fun with this challenge.

Support Students in Their Revision

Dear Teacher,

I come from a nontraveling family, so I am amazed that I've visited not only Canada, Mexico, Spain, and Latin America, including Cuba, but also Finland, Germany, Greece, Pakistan, India, Japan. I wrote about some of those trips in *Nepantla: Essays From the Land in the Middle.* Let me tell you about the spring of 1993, when, thanks to a fellowship, a small group of us from the U.S. interested in education and cultural issues spent two and a half weeks in the People's Republic of China. I traveled the long air miles seeking to see and begin to understand that ancient, resilient civilization, land of proverbs: "Water can drip through stone." "Beware the person with the Buddha's mouth and the snake's heart." I heard sayings about us too. "If you are in China for three days, you can write a book; one month, an article; but if you spend a year, you can write nothing, overwhelmed by our complexities." Isn't that true of any society? Understanding is a slow process.

Visiting city schools, we met dutiful students, standing shyly, folded into themselves, eyes cast down, learning English with the British accents of their teachers. Always respectful, the students brimmed with questions and curiosity, hoping to visit the U.S., America, *Mei guo,* literally, beautiful country.

At a preschool in a rural village, we sat in tiny green wooden chairs at children's tables and met with kindergarten teachers. Windows and doors filled with the round, curious faces—the children who usually sat in the room. Little booklets, "diaries," hung from strings on the wall, and student photographs hung from the ceiling on colored strands above the cold cement floor. These teachers, all women, worked closely with parents in this village. Both parents and teachers completed report cards on the children, and then they met and discussed the progress of the child, their shared concern. Parents as partners, members of the educational team.

The humorous school experience of our trip was during home-stays in another rural village. As our bus arrived, the wind blew, the temperature dropped—and dropped. An unexpected cold front had swooped down, and during our two days with our gracious host family, we froze; the only heat in our bedroom, the bare light bulb. My roommates and I tried to convince ourselves that the bulb was radiating great quantities of warmth, but when we turned off the light, the last semblance of our heat myth, the cold seemed even more biting. We slept in our clothes. Between dreams, I touched my hair thinking that it had surely frozen. I covered my head with a towel. When we visited the village elementary school the next day, a teacher welcomed us into the room. Little ones huddled in coats and hats sat in chairs that lined the walls.

"Let us sing a song for aunties and uncles," the teacher said, "and then they will sing for you." Uh-oh. The children sang two melodies we recognized, "Jingle Bells" and "Frere Jacques," not my first musical surprise in China. (I'd heard "Fur Elise," the theme from "The Godfather," "Spanish Eyes," and Julio Iglesias crooning, "To All the Girls I've Loved Before.")

We clapped enthusiastically and gazed into the children's expectant faces. Our group held a quick, whispered consultation, and then we raised our unaccustomed voices and laughingly began the great American classic "Old McDonald Had a Farm." Luckily, that was before people were videotaping everything. For our next number, we represented our country with yet another example of musical sophistication. To distract our young audience and conceal our lack of vocal ability, we boldly added movement to our performance. We made a large circle with the children and proceeded to sing "The Hokey Pokey," as our guides and the teachers laughed at our antics. We felt like clumsy giants as we "shook it all about" in the cold classroom but enjoyed the pleasure of being part of a circle with children. Such situations force us to at least briefly revise our view of ourselves.

That evening, as we walked to the community meeting place along poplar-lined roads, I looked up into the dark sky and resisted crying out at the size of the stars, the white light almost audible. More performances. Groups of children and adults danced and sang for us. When our guides were asked to perform, to my amazement, they rose and with no preparation unselfconsciously sang.

What next? You know. Slowly we realized that in this spirit of hospitality and generosity, our turn too must come. We squirmed, whispered to find songs we might all know, returned to our theme song and gathered the little ones for another round of putting "our left hand in."

Later, "Grandmother" came upstairs and motioned us to follow her to the family's room off the kitchen, where the family slept and watched their small black-and-white television. We enjoyed small bags of pumpkin seeds. A few months before, I'd spent two nights in a small home in Honduras and likewise watched TV with a family, enjoyed cookies and candy purchased from a nearby stand. In Honduras, I'd communicated easily with the family in Spanish; in China, all I had to offer my hosts were nods of appreciation, smiles, "*xiexie*" (shi-eh, shi-eh), thank you, thank you. Being in China unable to read any sign or hear familiar sounds except from our group, I again experienced the journey immigrants make. As tourists, we leave, taking facts, memories, images, impressions, stories. We're protected by our translators and guides.

I went to China from a society that values individualism, that repeats to itself that it is "the real thing," the most economically developed country in the world. China's present and past emphasizes collectivism. Surname is said or written first, revealing the importance of social relationships and ties, the high value placed on family obligations. Adults are aunts and uncles to little ones, and older people are grandmother or grandfather, connectedness steadily reinforced. We tend to be a country of nuclear families that can sometimes quickly distance ourselves physically and emotionally even from our neighbors.

When I was leaving Tiananmen Square, the largest kite in the air, an immense dragon with a tail perhaps fifty feet long, came furling down. In no time, passersby had formed a long line and soon, with group effort and with some laughter, pushed that flying dragon, a totem for China, back up into the sky.

In *The Poetics of Space,* Gaston Bachelard says that, ideally, when we create, we surprise ourselves by seeing even our past in a fresh way—as I've savored the trip to China again in sharing it with you. We paint or write or arrange the photographs of our travels or of our academic year to reexperience the sights and pleasures, but at a deeper level, we seek to feel the insights, the bits of wisdom that shook us, to jar them loose that they might move us again.

The Talmud reminds us, "We do not see things as they are; we see things as we are." Travel and learning from our diverse friends and teachers can help us "see" with deeper understanding. Are we willing to risk occasional embarrassment to connect with our students, their families, our peers? We need to know ourselves as cultural and creative beings first, know our values and style, before we can fully assess the serious but joyful work ahead. You're certainly a beacon—inspiring students, their families, and your peers with your determination to value each student and to set high standards for educational success, to be the necessary guide.

Teachers today stress the process of revision, but how many are engaged in that writing practice themselves? With rare exceptions, the only students I've met who enjoyed the process were already experienced writers. Beginning writers often feel that it was hard enough completing the assignment once. To return to that site of agony or at least discomfort seems boring, a total waste of time, masochistic. Many also argue that their work is fine and really the best they can do. Some will be satisfied with a *C*. Others secretly or not so secretly long for an *A+*. I did.

During my school years, I wanted teachers to approve of me and my work. Those were the days before revision was incorporated as a regular part of the writing process. I doubt that I would have enjoyed it then. Reaching the appropriate word length was never easy, probably my attraction to writing poetry.

What about you? Were you asked to revise throughout your school career, and if so, did you relish the experience?

Students in creative writing classes, particularly high school students, if they trust us, pour their intense feelings on the page, their loves, hates, angers. "But why should I have to revise?" they scowl. "That's exactly the way I feel. That's what I want to say, and I like the way it sounds. I don't want to change a word. I read it to my friends, and they really like it." They look at me sure that I couldn't possibly understand. Anyway, I'm some kind of alien. Didn't I just admit that I like revision? Their teachers have conspired to bring in support from the outside, and sure enough, when they glance at their teacher's faces, the teachers smile, agreeing with me.

I openly admit to them that I didn't always feel this way. I try to distinguish between writing for school or the public, and private writing that can indeed remain exactly as the author first wrote it. With adults no longer in school, I distinguish in similar ways between private writing and writing for an audience whether for publication, a gift, or a presentation.

I try to meet students where they are emotionally, developmentally, linguistically. Your task is infinitely harder. You're teaching a group and much as you try to individualize instruction, you are to prepare them to prove their competencies. To engage in meaningful revision (not just finding a synonym), whether it's writing for a test or for creative expression, students need strategies, a process, and confidence. In concrete ways, you build their courage.

We can support our students to repeat the practices of valuing their creative potential, remembering the necessity of quiet and of gathering their materials—their experiences and imagination, writing regularly, and revising. To help them to understand purpose, audience, tone, as I've suggested previously, use your own work to teach the revision process. Depending on the level of the students, use a sentence, paragraph, or longer passages to reveal how a writer improves her work. Use writers you admire and have students explore their own versions of a piece, variations on a theme. As poet Mary Oliver asks, why do we see art students sketching at museums and not writing students examining and trying what others have achieved? I well know it can be a struggle to find a positive comment to make on some papers, but pretend it was written by a favorite young person in your life. It's hard to build without a foundation of hope. Can a student try if he doesn't know the next steps, feels he can't succeed? Because of our knowledge, training, and experience, we can intervene with constructive, specific suggestions.

Donald Graves, such an important educator in the process of teaching writing, advises that in a conference with a student, we "lean back" at times and let the student lead. A return to the habit of listening. Because time is limited, coach your students to respond to one another's work in pairs and small groups. This requires training your class to be candid yet constructive editors. Our goal is to help students experience the pleasure of seeing their work improve. No one wants to be a bad writer, not really. Steadily, we're aiding students to experience the connection between reading and writing and the connection between concentration and imagination. Writers sit like the alert and patient frog poised to pounce on the right word, a fresh idea, a new solution to the puzzle. Yum! We're intrigued not oppressed. In spite of test pressure, how do we coax and coach our students to at least occasionally experience the difference? In part, we must experience it first.

I probably began being an advocate when I became a university administrator and began initiating local outreach programs to women and underserved populations. Since founding Día, the family literacy initiative, in 1996, I've learned that advocacy—whether for environmental, health, community, or educational issues—is incredibly hard work. The educators I most admire are advocates. Assisting students to practice revising their writing and, sometimes, their view of themselves is part of our work.

To reach our promise as a nation, we need to develop the talents of our all our students including those who are multicultural, multilingual. They also deserve a demanding education that connects them with their world. There are not enough gates or guards to protect us from the reality that we are all interconnected. Reducing educational inequities enriches individuals and communities, diminishes violence, increases collaboration, prepares us to think in more complex ways.

Back to "The Hokey Pokey." Are your fellow teachers determined to connect with diverse students and families, willing to revise their attitudes and strategies they may resisted in the past (dancing not required though sometimes helpful)? I sense a change as Texas librarians tell me that they want to be able to use bilingual books with their students and want their children and "grandbabies" to learn Spanish. Perhaps they've discovered the beauty of the language. They may also be aware that by 2050, demographers predict that about one-third of the U.S. population will be Latino.

Because teaching days can be so busy with students and required paperwork that there's little time to interact with peers, teachers mention their feelings of isolation. Personalities and value differences, as well as negative competition, can impede the serious and necessary work: creating staff communities that model our stated goals. Creative educators nurture healthy communities of learners who are readers, thinkers, and leaders working together both for their own well-being and for the good of students and their families.

Teachers who are part of a minority in the faculty, ethnic or otherwise, can also feel isolated. We all belong to various communities, not one. I'm a member of the community of daughters, mothers, aunts, sisters, wives, friends, teachers, writers, speakers, advocates, readers, cooks, gardeners, walkers, Latinas, and huggers, to name a few. Sometimes, though, we've learned how to hide the isolation we feel. I remember a Latina teacher at a Houston private school viewed as extremely cheerful by her colleagues. They were stunned when during my visit, she started crying. "It's painful being the only one of your kind," she said. That day, she didn't have to be the one Latina representing her ethnic group.

Our students can feel that way, too. "Will anyone look like me?" a child asks the first day of school. I meet African American and Latino students at private schools who say they feel burdened, asked to represent their group, expected to be experts on their culture's history, beliefs, and traditions. It's easy to forget the diversity in any group. Latinos, for example, include numerous races, religions, and home countries. Such students at prestigious universities say, "I hate it when everyone turns and looks at me when anything about diversity is mentioned in class." "Why do campuses like this play the game of 'we have a diversity of viewpoints'? Aren't they just avoiding the lack of minority students?" But times are changing.

Many teachers and administrators who are bilingual were themselves punished for speaking their home language at school. They speak of being yelled at for not following directions when they simply didn't understand what their teachers were saying. I've heard metropolitan district administrators remember the suffering, the panic, the fear of their accents, the struggle to survive. They were wounded psychologically and physically, passed over for honors, opportunities, encouragement, told, "You can't be an engineer." Dear teacher, you are part of the necessary change.

Although we can work to create classrooms welcoming to all, we can also increase our impact by being active in creating inclusive schools. We begin by knowing and trusting one another. Is your faculty a community? One activity that I participated in and now often use with groups is having them introduce themselves to someone they don't know well in the group by using family names. I might say, "I'm Pat Mora the daughter of Raúl and Estela Mora. My grandparents were . . ." Soon there's plenty of talking in the room. People learn about a colleague and inevitably find connections. A family history project can also be an interesting way for a school community or a group of teachers who wish to become better acquainted.

Seed, labyrinth, earth, feather, water—our symbol for creating our reservoirs and guiding our students to create theirs. We practice supporting students and peers in revising their work and their images of themselves. It's tiring and requires courage to be an articulate advocate for your students in your school, district, community, and professional organizations, but if not you, who? As Gandhi's said, "You must be the change you wish to see in the world."

Tips

Students and peers may need you to support them at times. Both groups can be discouraged by negative attitudes. By tapping your reservoirs of knowledge and commitment, you can steadily be a force for positive change. What are your three personal challenges to viewing yourself as a leader?

Incorporate your own and your student's varying journeys—some from down the block and some from far away—into your curriculum, encouraging students to build on what they and their families have learned. Assisting any group of students or faculty to create a learning community in which difference is respectfully accepted is a major challenge. We're preparing citizens to be part of a civil and just society though. We set the example. "As is the gardener, such is the garden." Remain unwilling to ignore a cruel remark. Surround yourself with colleagues who have better things to do than gossip and gripe. How do you and your peers support new, dedicated teachers?

Exploration for You

Since I've been writing about revising and seeing again, how do you "see" your school? How do you see your place in it? Is there a role you'd like to take and haven't?

I send along some questions that I hope you will find intriguing, that might help you review your school or campus, local community, and our national progress in creating inclusive instructional spaces. I also hope the questions will intrigue you to ponder your role in the process: past, present, and future. Interested in the habit of expanding our joint work, I hope you will share the questions and your own wise thoughts with colleagues and that discussions and explorations will continue. Ours, dear teacher, is an unending conversation because we continue to learn together.

QUESTIONS FOR REFLECTION

1. Am I an active part of creating an inclusive school, library or campus community, a community in which each person is valued?

2. Have I assessed my own heritage? Have I assessed the assumptions and values that emerge from my personal history?

3. Have I assessed the cultural backgrounds of the staff and students?

4. Have I acknowledged my need to continue learning about our human diversity and the need to dignify the cultures, languages, and homes of my students?

5. If I work with young students, do I encourage participation by all parents/families—including non-English-speaking parents and parents with limited economic means—in the educational experiences of their children?

6. Do I avoid defining culture only as the four *F*s: food, folklore, fashion, and festival?

7. Do I create a classroom climate in which no culture dominates, in which all languages are valued, in which varying learning styles are encouraged?

8. Do I provide varied reading and writing experiences that reflect local, regional, and national diversity and international voices?

9. Do I select diverse curriculum materials for authenticity, materials that reflect cultural complexities rather than reinforce stereotypes?

10. In reflecting on my campus or school, do I believe that our classrooms, library, and school/campus equally reflect the contributions of this country's many heritages?

11. Do my colleagues and I prepare students to participate actively in our pluralistic democracy?

Invitation to Write

Write a letter to yourself from a place you've visited, focusing on what was different from your daily life and how you felt about that difference.

Using a diary form, write about your family's first memories in this country. Assume the persona of one of your relatives and write in the first person. If you are trying to interest your students in collaborative projects, with a fellow writer, visual artist, or musician, you could illustrate the process.

A school mural could inspire a collection of family, neighborhood, or community stories and history. What about combining a mural with collaborative text? What about a collaborative mural of a vision for the future for your school? What has been the vision and does it need revising?

Does your faculty work well enough together that all or a group of you would consider a collaborative poem or writing project, occasionally braiding your voices?

CHAPTER SIX

Share Your Creations

Dear Teacher,

I love the scent of incense. Why don't I light it more often? Smelling it and watching the smoke rise and curl reminds me of seeing smoke ribbons rise every morning the weeks my husband and I were in Bali during the summer of 1997. (In the official language, Bhasa Indonesian, the accent falls on the last syllable, bah-LEE.) The length of time it took to arrive halfway around the globe made my body feel creased and crumpled even with a brief stop in Hawaii. When we finally arrived in Bali, we walked around trying to take in the abundance of hibiscus and bougainvillea, the botanical paradise where life sprouts exuberantly. We admired the carefully groomed layers of Balinese rice terraces, but as so often happens with considerable jet lag, our spirits didn't feel at home in our bodies for days. By then we'd put on the necessary sarongs and attended shadow puppet performances at open-air temples, watched the wide-eyed Legong dancers.

We'd walked into the nearby town of Ubud, along the way noticed small, green squares called *canang sari,* "morning offerings," made of strips of palm. The women who made the containers placed fresh flowers; a small mound of rice; perhaps, beans or chopped apples; and a stick of incense, the smoke scenting the air in front of homes and businesses.

The spiritual element was visible and daily present in Bali. To bless the computers and anthropological equipment my husband and his colleagues would use in their water projects, a temple priest dipped blooms in water that he then sprinkled lightly on the equipment. He explained a few rituals, explanations difficult to grasp fully because of language differences. He mentioned that the incense and flowers symbolized nourishing the spirit; and the bits of rice, and beans or apples, symbolized nourishing the body; the symbols daily offered to God. Incense and offerings were believed to lure and appease good and bad spirits daily.

"Don't run away from the spirit. Don't be too proud. There's a power behind you," the priest explained adding that just as rice seed put in the ground rises willingly; rice is placed on the forehead at a blessing in the hope that what we too will also grow.

Because I started writing somewhat late in my life and feel there's such a need for books by Latinas, I've rarely taken even a day off between book projects. I'd arrived in Bali discouraged at trying to place manuscripts, though, so I'd decided to read and take notes, my first break in years. In my journal, I wrote, "What life have I invented for myself and is it the right life? Have I been my full self? In what ways am I rich?" The questions return, of course, as they do for all of us. I derive such deep pleasure from writing, speaking, advocacy—a life without financial security, medical, or retirement benefits but with great personal benefits.

Developing our creative talents requires commitment as do parenting, fitness, professional progress, mindful living. Choosing the time alone to imagine and invent allows us to give and share a different part of ourselves whether we're musicians, mathematicians, composers, singers, dancers, biologists, playwrights. Once you have work to share, what prompts you to risk the sharing?

My travels whether foreign or national help me and sometimes force me through my senses to expand my options for writing, living, understanding. Mornings in Bali, I stared out from our small veranda at a rice paddy, pink with dawn. Mount Agung rose in the distance. With white clouds clustering around it, it looked like a soft blue mound. When the sky turned peach, the mountain disappeared into the clouds to brood for the day. Two water buffalo pulled a farmer's plow through the muddy paddy, *slosh, slosh, slosh.* The farmer in his sarong, T-shirt, and straw hat called out, *"Agg-Ta-Ta!"* I'd chat with Gusti, who worked at the small hotel and wanted to practice his English.

"Please enjoy your read," he would say when he saw me with a book. Every morning I'd see new, lovely offerings placed around the hotel. To begin a day by quickly creating beauty to share seemed a good practice. I kept seeing the beautiful little offerings made daily by local women in both simple and elaborate designs. How could I learn to make them when I didn't even speak the language? Again, I was hoping to use my hands rather than my head.

One day, I braved the fastest and shadiest route to Ubud from our hotel through a park called "the monkey forest." I tried not to make eye contact with the bold monkeys eager to pounce on tourists. By the time I arrived at the narrow, congested streets noisy with motor scooters, shopkeepers calling out, *"Haloo, haloo,* morning price, morning price," I was melting. At a women's art cooperative, I met a young saleswoman and asked how the offerings were made

"My sister and mother teach you," said Putu.

"Oh no," I said. "They don't even know me."

"Yes, yes," she said insistently. "No problem, no problem." She wrote down the address and motioned where I should go. Could I really walk down the street and through houses in an area I knew nothing about and in which I really couldn't communicate, I wondered. (I knew what my grown children would think of this idea.) But I really did want to try making the small green palm squares filled with flowers, appeasements through nature, sights and scents to pacify evil spirits and to welcome good ones. The Balinese seek balance. I suspected patience would be required, not my strength as you know, but off I went.

Of course, people stared at the woman peering at the addresses and obviously not Balinese. After a few wrong turns and following the sound of chickens as directed, I saw two women sitting and chatting on the floor of a raised porch watching TV.

"Nama saya Pat," I said introducing myself and trying to explain that Putu had sent me. The daughter Made (MAH deh) spoke less English than I'd hoped, and Sari, her mother, who had never been to school, spoke only Balinese, and thus, the few Indonesian words I knew had to be translated by her daughter or husband. I began my hand movements; it was like a game of charades. We communicated with gestures and facial expressions and tried my small dictionary, but as happens around the world (in schools and libraries too) when a common language isn't shared, smiles and laughter were a good bridge.

Sari, who quickly grasped what intrigued me, had her daughter bring a fresh palm leaf off the roof. Sari picked up her knife and began to cut, fold, and notch the palm. In a matter of minutes, she had made a green square to hold the offerings. Although the *canang sari* could be bought at the market, many women still took pride in making their own. Like Mexican bakers who carry many recipes in their heads, Sari could make design after design, her knife and rough hands creating beauty in minutes. I sat there laughing with delight, marveling at all her hands made.

Sari then pointed at me signaling that I should try. Trouble ahead. My sad attempts proved a source of great hilarity for the three of us. Sari was a patient teacher. At anything I did even remotely right, she and Made would clap and say with great enthusiasm, *"Bagus! Bagus!"* (bah GOOS) meaning "beautiful, beautiful." Sari sent me home with some palm.

"I will practice," I said. "Practice, practice," they chimed. I agreed to return and to help Made with her English. I sat on our hotel veranda with my palm and scissors, a knife not even a possibility. I read my scribbled notes and studied my indecipherable drawings. My hands felt clumsy, and I thought of the many clumsy beginnings my hands had experienced: holding a pencil, caring for a baby, cooking, gardening, writing. With age, we can almost savor the awkwardness knowing what practice can yield.

I liked the smell of the leaf when I cut it, the idea of creating something fresh, and I found the ephemeral nature of the offerings and their receptacles a good life lesson. What we make is seldom timeless—nor are we.

When Medae, the wife of our hotel owner, learned of my interest, she began sending elaborate offerings for my room, the generosity of strangers. I never ceased to be amazed at the casual way the flowers we pamper were treated in Bali. Fresh hibiscus were put in vases in our room—without water—since the lush blooms would be replaced the following day. I wondered if I stood still long enough if *I,* too, would sprout and bloom on that island garden. Madae's offerings came filled with hibiscus, bougainvillea, brown and chartreuse spider orchids. She enjoyed sharing what she made, and I was the fortunate recipient. She brought me a small stapler because she was afraid I'd scar my hands putting the offerings together with thin, traditional pieces of bamboo.

Madae explained that smoke from the incense helps our relationship with God. The deep premise that all begins with God explained the morning rituals of making an offering and putting it out to protect the places that mattered to a woman, that were important to her sense of identity. Madae would gently push the incense smoke up toward heaven and then she would bathe her face with it.

One night I watched a full moon, a gold round, floating behind our room in the rice paddy's silver water. I think back now, dear teacher, to my days there, surrounded by such diverse, thriving plant life, and I think of the full blossoming of our complex selves, of how we each can be a stunning light if we but take the risk. I think about loyalty to diversity—in the environment, in ourselves, our family, place of work, community, all the communities around our globe.

Steve, an anthropologist friend who has worked in Bali for years, invited me to give a poetry reading and had the invitation carved into a lontar palm, an ancient custom. Such special gifts—the many traditional offerings simple and elaborate. The lessons were also gifts. I continued taking notes and trying to make the offerings. I thought about the daily rituals in my life and about that notion of adding what we've made, a bit of beauty, to the world. I listened to the palm fronds, watched their shadows on the wall.

Shadows fascinate me. What fascinates you, intrigues you to research or draw, to share what you discover, invent? Mom was fond of quoting from the Parable of the Talents, "To whom much is given, much is expected." To avoid sharing our creative talents, do we minimize them, not sing though we have a good voice? Remember the lilac bush? By repeating our usual, often repressive routines, do we keep our internal light dim?

By writing to you, I'm sharing what I do. I remember Lobo, my aunt, making shadow figures with her hands on the wall by our beds. Little rabbits appeared, and my sister Cissy and I giggled with delight. I watched tree shadows sway in my childhood backyard and anticipated the afternoon shadows that slid over the mountain, a bare mountain in the center of my hometown. In Santa Fe, I watch shadows on adobe, the afternoon shadows of quaking aspens whose Latin name I so like, *Populus tremula*. Sometimes I think of the shadows on the wall as the breaths of beings who once climbed the hills. The shadows mesmerize like smoke does, real and yet illusory, eluding everything but my patience. "To pay attention, this is our endless / and proper work," writes Mary Oliver.

Balinese women began their day by giving. What gifts do you and I bring? Wanting to share what we have, what we've made, is a human impulse that comes from caring. How do we share, grateful for the bounty we've received, continuing the circle of receiving and giving? I want to share both the literacy that has given me so much pleasure, and what I write, the lines I revise and polish.

I hadn't thought about it before, but writing is in a very specific way a handmade gift, isn't it? The hand presses words into a page. Computers do diminish the need to hand make every page of course. I'm reminded of the young writer in Michigan's Upper Peninsula who asked me how long it took me to make all the copies of my books and how I managed to make the cover so firm. I relish children's literal questions.

I'm proposing sharing what we create in informal and personal ways rather than only focusing on publication, performances, art shows, often far too great a focus for young people. Watching the Balinese women was a kind of induction into the world of art making, the movement away from making our poem or ceramic bowl only for ourselves to floating it out in the world, less ego attachment, less ego risk. We can agree to plan or to participate in a reading or a photography exhibit or prepare our work as a gift—a poem for a niece's wedding ceremony, a family history given at Thanksgiving, a painting for graduation.

When my younger sister, Stella, turned fifty, I decided to put together a book of family messages to her. Stella is inordinately thoughtful and generous, so we all had memories to share and gratitude to express. I wrote the family and sent them each parchment paper and instructions, and I found a young woman with a fine collection of dried flowers who created the cover. I enjoyed both writing a poem for Stella and, because she has always loved to sing, writing a song to her set to "When Irish Eyes Are Smiling," a song we sang often in grade school. For us, I had to alter the song's cultural history.

Stella's Song

(Old Irish-Mexican Tune)

When Stel-la's eyes are smil-in,

Sure, it's like the de-sert sun. . . .

Such lighthearted sharing can delight the giver and the receiver.

Teachers belonging to a writing group may volunteer to read for a faculty event or team up with a friend or colleague working in another medium to present a music and poetry event, for example.

Does planning such an event or agreeing to participate make you nervous? Don't let that stop you. Some very experienced and accomplished artists always feel that discomfort. When we share our work we validate it, and we learn from hearing it and from watching others respond to it. We also inspire others to dare.

Try not to focus on that pesky ego but on a spirit of generosity, the artistic harvest that like any harvest is meant to be shared. Think of the wonder of autumn. In Santa Fe, the world turns gold from the chamisa, aspen, and cottonwoods releasing their final display before they rest. New Mexico sunflowers, purple asters and the seed flags of blue grama grass glisten in the morning dew and sway in the afternoon sunlight. I feel my skin stretch to contain the pleasure, earth's ripeness. You too must feel the joy of the harvest when you see the students you've prepared moving on and excelling.

The philosopher Heidegger wrote that we are born twice, the second time by the strength of our own courage. It's natural and healthy to want to share what we've worked on—a booklet, cake, flower arrangement, painting, poem—and the practice often allows us to see or hear areas of our work that need fine-tuning. Although I read a poem aloud through its many revisions, it is often when I share it with a group that I may discover or have reconfirmed my hunch that certain lines need more work. We also enjoy the pleasure of approval and, at times, of being of use to others, all strong incentives that help us want to generate new work. And why not share what you discover, what delights or intrigues or troubles or angers you? Come on. Enrich us.

Pursuing what intrigues me—new poetic forms or new plant names—also excites me and makes my fingers itch to be writing again. I prize Chilean Pablo Neruda, ambassador and poet who, when he received the Nobel Prize in 1971, said that a poet must achieve balance "between solitude and solidarity, between feeling and action." I smile that he also said that he had no idea how to define poetry; he only knew that it is "dark" and "dazzling." Reading about him, I learned that in the 1950s, he wrote more than 200 odes to be printed in the newspaper. Striving for clear, accessible language, he wrote long, skinny poems, exuberant swooshes of praise for the often ordinary things he loved: handmade slippers, saltshakers, tomatoes. In the odes, eventually published in four volumes, we hear the gentle humor of Neruda's voice, almost that of a doting parent who cherishes each object. I was compiling my first collection of teen poems then and decided to write an "Ode to Pizza." Eventually, I wrote the poetry collection *Adobe Odes,* praise songs to things I love: tulips, sunflowers, guacamole. I hoped others, like you, might then want to write your odes, add your voices, praising, praising the "ordinary" wonders of the planet. Also, the not so ordinary—like readers.

Without you

what I've prepared will wither

into dust.

Tempt you?

"Ode to Readers," *Adobe Odes*

Like flowers, poems are wonderful to share. Too often teachers at all levels are far more interested in having students write poetry than in writing it themselves. When I ask why, teachers mention negative memories, being asked what poems meant, and feeling that their own work never satisfied a teacher.

Poetry won't make anyone a best seller or a household name, but it can improve any writer's work, give a writer great joy, and is an appreciated gift. When is the last time you wrote a poem? Poetry is an invitation to explore as is all writing, but it's an invitation to shape language for the greatest effect. Writing poetry, we ponder and plunge deep into words, follow their path often without a deep narrative concern. Poetry is also a call and a comfort to the self and to others. In the words of the Greek poet George Seferis, poetry is "strong enough to help."

And help we need on our occasionally lonely and discouraging journey, even those of us with many blessings. Some suggestions for trying poetry: sample an array of poets and find a few who appeal to you. Spend time reading their work. What is it that you enjoy about it? Do you like set rhyme and meter, free verse, a mix of styles?

Now, I'm going to urge you to try some odes or whatever kind of poetry appeals to you. Try writing at least one poem in the style of a poet you liked. Consider sharing this draft with someone you trust. I'd avoid focusing on whether your reader liked your poem or not. Ascertain if the poem intrigued your reader, what line or lines most appealed to her, what opportunities might you have missed. In a relaxed fashion, also try a few poems perhaps exploring telling a story with economy or asking yourself to focus more on pacing, mood, and word choice than you might in prose. Try rhyme.

Seeds, labyrinth, sand, feather, water. I send you an imaginary packet of incense. It reminds me of the glow and comfort of fire, of a gentle wind, of connecting with a power greater than ourselves, of cultivating generosity about what we explore and create, about releasing a part of ourselves that we're allowing to emerge.

Exploration

Design a wordless, symbolic offering, religious or personal.

Inspired by installation art, present a piece of your writing in some nonstandard way—in a box, perhaps enhanced by symbols or *recuerdos*, mementos, photographs, flowers; or as a container for blossoms, as part of a collage, laminated and covered by water.

Invitation to Write

Write about a trip real or imagined that replenished your spirit and prompted you to share discoveries or gifts. What were the necessary elements that renewed you?

Write about your motivations for creating your offering.

Write and share an ode or a set of odes about concrete objects that delight you.

Create Sharing Opportunities for Students

Dear Teacher,

I enter a high school English classroom and quickly sense anticipation. The teacher welcomes me warmly and says that her students have looked forward to sharing their poems with me. I don't remember the name or location of the school, but do I remember those students—and their teacher.

How did she gain the trust of her class, guide each student to see the strength in his writing, build the group spirit evident as students volunteered to share their work? I wasn't seeing the teens often negatively depicted on the media, the stereotypes that seldom do justice to the young people I care about and that the teacher cared about. She'd taught her students to experiment with language and listen to one another with respect. They had practiced for my visit and took pride in one another as they volunteered to stand and read. Their teacher stood quietly on the sidelines conveying her interest and pride in each reader. By creating a space in which her students safely shared what they created, an enthusiastic and talented teacher watched her pupils sing out their words. Reading poems they'd revised, the students were also revising their opinion of themselves and of one another.

An unprepared high school audience can be among the most challenging. Teens can need the approval (or disapproval) of their peers, and in large group situations, they can feel it's "cool" to resist hearing the presenter—and I don't mean a volume issue. Of course, when teachers have connected my writing to the lives of their students, teens can be an energetic audience and ask intriguing writing questions. The popularity of poetry slams, spoken word, or open-mike events now provide a space for students to share their work and hear their voices valued, though for some, sharing and discussing their work in small groups or with selected audiences may be most satisfying. I'll confess that though I've always enjoyed public speaking, I would never have been a poetry-slam type.

I was excited to learn that every high school in Greensboro, North Carolina, now has a poet laureate. When I asked the students why they'd decided to compete by submitting their poems, I learned from listening to this diverse group—the Russian girl who felt embarrassed that she, whose first language wasn't English, had been selected; the athletes who found a pleasant humor in being jocks and poets, surprising their peers. I was reminded of the teens who had read at the Heard Museum in Phoenix years ago, invited to write in English or their home language. Wonderful invitation. One student performed her poem in sign language. All the poems were translated into English as needed, but it was a memorable experience to see young people smiling at their families and teachers as they read their poems in the language of their hearts, a multilayered experience for us all. Again, they had been prepared to succeed at the microphone, a skill that also improves with practice and can become pure pleasure.

Such experiences help students realize that their voice, their work matters, that it is relevant. Hearing themselves and one another can make their voices and their past useful, a valued part of the community's public history, its many narratives. What a strong incentive for revision and for new work. We all need an audience.

Many elementary students are eager to share what they've memorized or written and also learn poise and self-confidence from sharing. Recently, on a Día visit to Durham, North Carolina, I watched second graders perform for their schoolmates and me. Their young teacher, full of excitement, settled her eager students at the front of the cafetorium. She moved to the side (I love to watch teachers watch their students perform), nodded, and gave them a big smile. From memory, those cute students surprised me by reciting *Book Fiesta: Celebrate Children's Day/Book Day, Celebremos El día de los niños/El día de los libros* in English *and* Spanish. What a moment as I watched and listened, thought about Día's goals of connecting children to books, languages, and cultures. The audience and I clapped and clapped as we did for another class that had memorized haiku from *¡Yum! ¡MmMm! ¡Qué rico!* I told the students that they were smarter than I was. I would have needed to look at my books.

The art teacher had worked with her classes to create wonderful murals inspired by the art of Rafael López. When I cautiously asked the teacher about possible conflicts given the current emphasis on testing, she forcefully responded that education is about problem solving whether the students are taking an exam or determining the dimensions and materials needed for their creative work. Such mentors, dear teacher, make me want to rush home and write you a letter.

Just as we can be nervous about sharing our work, some students may seek to avoid the exposure. In working with them, we discover their talents and stories, all they have to share. In creating such opportunities, we deepen our creativity as teachers whether it's work students memorized or created themselves. Maybe they share duets or choral reading they wrote and designed to present together.

Books and lists of techniques for sharing aren't hard to find, but where do we find the interest in each student, the determination (and energy) to draw the talent out? Young Author Days, author teas at which student authors enjoy autographing their book, and presentations by students and families who together created family oral histories can be extremely challenging to the organizers, but dedicated teachers see the impact on their students, the excitement and pride.

Through personal connections and establishing trust, teachers sense how best to assist a student to share with one student or the class; to stand and read at a library, bookstore, café; or to share work at a senior center. When we're designing safe sharing opportunities, we need to assess what hurdles each student might be confronting. To assist her to cross borders and build community, it's essential to be attentive to the details including the students' realities.

Our deepest resource for this complex work is ourselves if we've connected to the emotional knowledge we all need to be effective educators. How do you encourage each student to raise his unique voice, protecting his ego while helping him take a risk?

I begin with the premise that educators are leaders, and so imagine you creating opportunities for students, families, and your colleagues to share their creative work. It's rewarding to see students and their families succeed thanks to the wise assistance of educators and volunteers. I ache seeing families proud of their child who is speaking at the microphone, though he is speaking in a language the family can't understand. I smile when those parents and families are openly welcomed at the celebration, greeted by someone in their own language, as was a family from El Salvador at a large and fancy tea hosted by the Boston Public Library. The oldest son was to introduce me. The family and I were probably the only Latinos in the room, but organizers who proudly spoke Spanish made the family feel welcome. The student presenters, who mirrored Boston's diversity, had been coached to succeed. I watched the Latino family knowing the hard road ahead, how they might have wondered about what to wear and how to conduct themselves in a place of different cultural norms, but I felt so pleased that the library supporters had designed an author award event that succeeded at many levels. The students were the stars.

I'm sure that evening the tired, hardworking volunteers experienced the quiet satisfaction that's a reward of giving. I'm amazed at the generosity of literacy volunteers across the country who annually stage events that allow students and families to shine and receive applause.

Volunteers in all fields are eloquent about the great benefits they derive from their work. Because giving reinforces our sense of worth, it's important that all families have ways of strengthening a school or library in substantive ways. Philanthropy, as my wise friend Dan reminds me, is not only about money. That troublesome, mean-spirited monster, elitism fosters the belief that certain people are givers and others only capable of receiving.

Although parents may have always shared their culinary talents at elementary schools, parents with professional training have often been more visible in sharing their fund-raising or organizational skills. What a pleasure to see leadership programs for Spanish-speaking parents sponsored in Texas, to see a group of Spanish-speaking parents present a session titled, "Piñata de Cuentos," a piñata of stories. Working with a teacher, the parents had studied books in Spanish and bilingual books and then made posters about the books for their child's school. Not only did the parents' art decorate the halls, a fact that made the parents proud, but they'd also practiced presenting the book to their child's class.

In Maryland, a monolingual-English reading specialist started evening book clubs for parents who didn't speak English. Because she was patient and treated the adults with interest and respect, through translators including their children, the parents slowly began to tell her their lives and dreams as they saw the connections between the pages of picture books and their realities. "Soon they were connecting the books they were enjoying to their own lives and history, asking their children to translate the parents' stories about growing up. They had so much to share," the teacher confided. I still see this teacher, her face red, fighting back tears, when she talked about the profound connections established. I hear her sadness when she recounted that some of her fellow educators "just want those kids put in special ed." She saw the intelligence beneath the often demeaned exterior.

Her passionate commitment to her undervalued students reminded me of how moved I was years ago when I read Mina Shaughnessy's *Errors and Expectations*. Who among us hasn't seen educators falsely and sometimes cruelly assess a student's intelligence and potential based on her accent, skin color, economic status, previous educational opportunities, grammatical errors? And might we have done this too?

That Maryland reading teacher was overwhelmed by the generosity of the families who brought her the gifts they could. It's not the carefully wrapped candle from the dollar store that motivates such dedicated educators though.

In addition to creating opportunities for students—and if you're an elementary school teacher, to creating opportunities for families to share what they create—are you tempted to plan an occasion for peer or friend sharing? A few years ago, I invited some of my women friends to a gathering I called *Arte y Te,* art and tea. On the invitation, I asked guests to bring a piece of art they valued. The piece could be bought, found, or made. The items selected were as diverse as the guests, from pink roses to a cross-stitch made by my friend Carolyn's mother for her hope chest. The needle was still in the material. Sitting in a circle, our group all felt connected to this woman who had done her careful needle work in South Carolina years ago.

I subsequently gathered this group to talk about creativity. I savor the memories of that day, filling the house with fresh flowers and candles, covering the table with good food, colorful Mexican plates, and children's toys, designing the occasion for and with my friend Elizabeth. Supporting the creativity of others reinforces our own commitment to this aspect of our lives. We explored our obstacles and habits. Women spoke of the struggles to find time, to have a place for inventive work, the challenge of believing in the self. Having good friends was high on the list of inspirations and sustenance. Sharing, whether sharing ideas, stories, or work we've made, strengthens our resolve.

The enthusiasm of readers and listeners helps too. "So do you like it when kids read your books?" I love the energetic tone of the boy asking the question. You bet. It's a warm pleasure to imagine a child alone turning the pages of one of my books or a family or class reading the books together. As you've gathered, I also thoroughly enjoy reading my work to audiences of all ages. I may have a better time than they do. Unexpectedly, almost fifteen years ago now, I also became a literacy advocate for sharing what I now call bookjoy.

This part of my journey began on a spring morning in 1996 at the University of Arizona in Tucson. I've told the story often about being interviewed on the campus public radio station and for the first time hearing about the Mexican, April 30th celebration of *El día del niño,* the day of the child. Children annually look forward to *their* day that can include treats, picnics, and special performances often planned collaboratively by parents and teachers.

I'd heard children, including my own, ask, "Why do we have Mother's Day and Father's Day and not Kids' Day?" ZAP! What a great idea: annually celebrating children. A few minutes later, a second zap. What about linking the celebration to books? I've joked that I was "zapped by Día," as in given a jolt of excitement.

The family literacy initiative, *El día de los niños/El día de los libros,* Children's Day/Book Day, is now often known as "Día," which means "day" in Spanish. It's difficult to remember my pre-Día life. I'll bet it was more leisurely, less stressful.

I'd published a number of children's books by then and realized our literacy inequities as I traveled around the country. I love to read and wanted all our children to experience the pleasure and power of being readers. About 5,000 children's books are published in the U.S. each year, but they still don't reflect the rich diversity of our country. For example, though the Latino population is 15% of the country and though one in four children under the age of five is Latino, fewer than 2% of the children's books published annually are by or about Latinos.

Children need to see themselves in books, in the books their teachers and librarians share and discuss, and to see such books in their home, classroom, bookstore, and library. Although much is said and written about the availability of "multicultural" books, we have a long way to go before major publishers diversify their staffs and offer literature to all ages that reflects our resplendent diversity. We need those books for ourselves and for all students. We need them in public libraries, school libraries, class libraries, and home libraries. My friend Patricia adds, "And we need them for our inner libraries."

I've long quibbled with what I think is the incorrect use of the word "multicultural." Indeed the world and our country are multicultural, composed of people from many cultures. All books are "cultural" in that they are written by a particular person who is part of a culture, a set of traditions, values, ways of seeing the world, definitions of excellence, whether the author is Anglo American or Asian American. Like our families, cultures are complex, diverse, and dynamic, so we need many books to even begin to convey the lives of different cultural groups.

I also question the popular use of the word "mainstream." What does that *really* mean? Given our national plurality, the true mainstream is composed of our many ethnicities, isn't it?

Initially, the Día initiative was about an annual April 30th celebration. My friends and fellows booklovers, members of REFORMA (The National Association to Promote Library and Information Services to Latinos and the Spanish Speaking) became my first allies, literacy advocates like Oralia and Rose championing this initiative. Other librarians also helped to spread the concept, and teachers and community organizations caught the spirit.

I'm grateful to my young and wise friend Marta, a staunch Día and literacy advocate, who reminded me of the danger of privileging print literacy, of equating it with wisdom, for example.

Our vision began to grow. Yes, like writing, effective advocacy requires vision and revision, in this case, with our steadfast, collaborative allies. We learned that this work is really a daily commitment, and culminating celebrations of that commitment are now held across the country on or near April 30th. We began to promote family literacy and linking all children to books, languages, and cultures. Recently, I went to a community gathering at a park in Detroit. Organizers had planned a true family event at which thousands of books were given away and families enjoyed free puppet shows, games, face painting.

Schools and libraries begin planning their annual Día celebrations in the fall and now see the opportunity to build partnerships with diverse families, community organizations, local businesses, the media, and local and state elected officials. The Día committee plans events that focus on the importance of reading families and of school and public libraries. In Portland, Oregon last year, families who signed a reading pledge at the Día public library celebration received a free book to add to their home libraries. In various cities, students and volunteers of all ages prepare presentations for nearby elementary schools or assist with Día events, a community service opportunity. Many communities and libraries host book giveaways.

A bookstore in Denver sponsored a Mother-to-Mother Club at which women gathered to chat about books and varying cultural customs and then planned a Día event for their children. Essential to this work, says Elva, a fine librarian, is the willingness to form partnerships with the community, to look around the planning group and ask if everyone who needs to be included is present. She knows that

Día is creating an easy bridge for nontraditional library users to join the library family. My North Carolina library friends say Día = Diversity in Action and plan events to honor their local cultures and languages. Like those in Texas and California, North Carolina librarians are now promoting Día statewide. What other states and cities will join this initiative for sharing bookjoy? Yours?

Advocacy work is never done, but we're sustained by Cesar Chávez's hopeful, "*Sí se puede.*" Yes, we can. We can do this work. *Sí*, yes.

Bilingual books are often part of Día events. Most of our country's teachers and librarians don't speak Spanish, and some openly admit feeling nervous about using bilingual books and even about saying Día's full name. I appreciate that necessary candor because we can't assist our students if we don't know the impediments. Día is a good opportunity to honor linguistic wealth in our country, all the languages spoken. How I admire educators who leap into a foreign language to more effectively connect with their community.

Recently a young reporter asked, "What makes Día unique, different from other literacy celebrations?" Great question. Because literacy is essential in our democracy, Día is a daily call to action that emphasizes the importance of children, linking *all* children to books, languages, and cultures; the importance of children's books that reflect our national diversity; and also of parents and families as partners with libraries and schools in the literacy process of sharing bookjoy.

Even with the funding Día has received and the fact that it is now housed at the American Library Association, I've learned what you know if you've ever engaged in advocacy work. It's both gratifying and heartbreaking, especially if connecting and engaging with the underserved is a goal. Advocacy is incredibly hard work requiring inventive, enthusiastic, reliable, allies, and organizations committed to true collaboration and persistence. I'm amazed that to grow an active Día community requires this much effort, but since the concept bonked me on the head, I feel an unexpected responsibility. I'm grateful every year to all the committed supporters of children and books who create wonderful Día celebrations. Join us, dear teacher! Together, we're building a bridge on which traffic moves in both directions. Families come to libraries and schools, and teachers and librarians go out to serve families.

The Bookjoy Bridge

Together, *cada día,* every day,

we're building the bridge to bookjoy.

Young and old stroll across it chatting night and day.

Together, *cada día,* every day,

in many languages, library families say,

"Reading. A happy habit we enjoy!"

Together, *cada día,* every day,

you and I build the bridge to bookjoy.

Día is one occasion for students to stand and share work they've shaped or learned, where they practice being contributing members of their school and community. I send incense as a symbol of sharing what we create and as a reminder that by fostering such opportunities for writers and artists of all backgrounds and ages, we reinforce their ability to enrich their city. I wish we could talk more about how, as we do this challenging though rewarding work, we're also shaping ourselves.

Tips

Practice your creative advocacy by initiating or enriching a Día celebration in your community, by adding a new dimension. Remember that change is slow. It takes time and consistency to build trust.

Experiment with interesting juxtapositions and combinations to make literacy enjoyable. A small farmer's market in New Mexico has a "Biggest Vegetable and Best Poem Contest." Winning poems receive a ribbon and all poems are published in a book.

Watching jazz musicians perform and improvise, I've wondered about luring more students to sharing their work through small group presentations. Choral readings are popular, but I'm proposing students writing poems on an agreed-upon topic and then working on them together to be presented as a duet or having a group of students select a theme for their poems and then creating a group piece that could include music, sound, visual art. Shy students may find such group presentations a less threatening way to share their work, and students can learn from one another, refining their abilities to be attentive to rhythms and repetitions, to weaving their words and ideas together.

Exploration for You

If you and your colleagues at work exchange gifts, might you decide to exchange a small example of your creative work? I know what little free time librarians and teachers have, but by setting limits, might this prove a pleasant alternative?

If you teach elementary school students and have planned student or family sharing events in the past, have you been pleased with the family participation? Has a diverse group of parents helped plan the event?

Invitation to Write

Describe an early memory of sharing your writing or visual art. Write about what that memory can teach you about your work as an educator today.

Refresh yourself with visual art. Enjoy a book of images, photography, painting, and the like, perhaps from one of your students' cultural groups, and let the images serve as prompts for a poem.

CHAPTER SEVEN

Steadily Persist in Your Creative Work

Dear Teacher,

Me writing in an Italian castle? Can you imagine such an opportunity? I certainly couldn't until a bit of magic happened. A letter informed me that I'd received a Civitella Ranieri Fellowship to spend a few weeks writing in Italy—in a castle.

An extra bonus was that my husband, Vern, would accompany me and work on his projects too. En route to our writing adventure, we visited Rome where the sight and sound of grand fountains had particular appeal because a heat wave greeted us. In Venice, we rode the boats that function as buses down the green canals winding by two- and three-story houses painted the color of spices: paprika, mustard, and cinnamon. Our budget decreed pasta, pizza, and gelato, no low-carb diet.

The day we were to arrive at the castle, we took two trains to Perugia, a city in the center of the Italian peninsula. We looked out at the tall stone houses, the fertile fields of the high Tiber valley. The land-locked region of Umbria, our destination, is known as *il cuore verde d'Italia,* the green heart of Italy, and as the train rolled along past fertile fields and small kitchen gardens, we understood why.

Across from us on the first train sat a couple from Laredo, Texas, who had also discovered how helpful speaking Spanish is in Italy. Even though I practiced basic phrases in Italian and was grateful for the Italians who helped answer our questions, I felt the discomfort of not being able to express myself fully, clearly.

Literacy is power. I again thought of the many non-English-speaking residents in the U.S., particularly those without economic buffers.

The director of the Civitella Ranieri Foundation kindly met our train and drove us to *il castello d'Civitella,* the castle near Umbertide (oom BEHR tee deh). Our mouths gaped as we drove through the arch and the iron gates and gazed up at the massive stone structure and its two turrets. How could it be that we would live in a real fifteenth-century castle for five weeks? Ten fellows, many with strong, international connections—composers, visual artists, and writers—had been invited from around the world to come and focus on our work. I felt like the country mouse, well, the desert mouse. My husband was in castle heaven.

We lived in two large rooms on the third floor. Detail: Our shower was located in the center of one of the castle turrets. Out our narrow front window, swallows whistled and zipped right toward us and then at the last second veered off from the castle walls into great circles. The Ranieri family had lived in this area for 1,000 years. The first castle burned, and the present one was built a mere 500 years ago.

We wandered the dark halls and gawked at the wooden beams planed by hand, the old furniture, portraits of saints, of family members in armor with dates like 1296 and 1440, with names like Glotto, Franco, Valerio, Bernardino. We saw a full suit of armor, lances in the corners, fireplaces six-feet high, and two wall-size family trees with names—of men. We peered through glass into the locked library and its dusty books. Outside, massive terra-cotta urns were filled with red geraniums and purple petunias. When I looked up from the lawn out front, I saw the tiny turret window, our shower.

As always, I savored the landscape around me. The castle was in an area of dense forest, much of it now converted to fields. In every direction were grand trees, a patchwork of green and gold hills—corn, wheat, sunflowers. *Girasole* in Italian meaning sun turning, *mirasol* in Spanish meaning sun gazing, do indeed look like rows of attentive students staring devotedly at the sun. I remember first seeing their upturned faces all in the same direction in Spain years ago, something so touching about their open, unabashed craning that probably reminded me of my young self in elementary school.

At my writing table in the castle, I began the circular journey again, the practices I repeat in returning to writing: I worked at valuing my creative self, a challenge because I was living with very accomplished and talented people. I'd hear the pianist warming up.

Although the place and group could be intimidating, I reminded myself to value my time and not squander energy on self-doubt.

I'd been given solitude. Having my husband in the adjoining room wasn't a problem; we've done our work in close proximity for years. Cute as he is, though, I'd find working with him or anyone in the same room difficult. We all have our "tics," members of what my daughter Libby calls "special people clubs." I'd begun to gather ideas for a book on creativity for educators and to explore possibilities. Thinking of you, believing in the significance of your work, I thought about us having this conversation together. I also started poems knowing each of the residents would share some aspect of her work at the end of our time there.

Ode to Civitella

Follow the winding road

into the long-ago story.

Before sunrise, hear

the rooster, *fortissimo,*

free of our introspective frowns,

nourished

by the song he crows.

I decorated my table with a wheat sheaf from a nearby field; pinecones from an Italian cypress that reminded me of my childhood home in El Paso; a shiny chestnut; a small, white pitcher of flowers. I didn't feel brilliant or inspired the way I perceived those around me to be, but like the folk artists I admire who pick up a piece of wood to begin carving again, I calmly told myself that I must write what I could every day hoping that slowly I'd improve. Like many, I cherish the story about the gifted cellist Pablo Casals who at ninety still practiced four to five hours a day. Asked why, he responded that he thought he was improving.

I was anxious to listen to myself and to listen and learn from others, hear how those in different disciplines perceived their work. The word "discipline" can have such negative and rigid connotations, and yet I immediately sensed that each artist was committed to a schedule of work, willing to grope along in the unknown, each morning— a sigh and a hope.

To initiate a helpful routine, Vern and I began early morning walks to savor the cool air, the comfort of the rhythm and the bird and bug sounds. My work on *The Song of Francis and the Animals* was finished by then, but seeing the hills, the places he walked, hearing the cicada sounds he heard, I briefly encountered deep listening, being attentive enough that fleetingly I could hear the light song of a rock, a bloom, a toad—their internal song, the earth's symphony below audible sounds.

What is your song, dear teacher, the one deep within you? What is mine? And what is the song of each of our students?

Before going to Civitella, I'd made some notes on the earth's music, rain playing the wood slats of the ramada in the Santa Fe garden as if they were a marimba, the refreshing splash of fountains, but I hadn't sensed the earth's undersong. Am I willing to practice enough solitude to drink from that musical well?

A few cats wandered the grounds, and although I had no intention of beginning a new children's book and, in fact, had left the States discouraged at how difficult it remains to place manuscripts for children, I began playing with the words "the castle cat, the castle cat." I couldn't resist playing with assonance: *cat, path, fast;* and then, I began creating a series of vignettes about a little fellow and his daily (mis)adventures. Children love castles and cats, I reasoned. Maybe the extended poem could find a home. I wrote the first draft, deciding on three-line verses glued together by assonance rather than a set rhyme. I began the fun of revision, thrilled like a child discovering a shiny rock each time I thought of a word with the *A* sound.

> Oh, have you seen the castle cat,
>
> the castle cat that ambles down the leafy path
>
> sniffing an adventure?

Wish the project luck, *buona fortuna.*

When I thought of ending these letters with the practice of persistence, I had in mind rhythms, rituals, reservoirs, rejuvenation. In spite of the heat, being at the castle was an unexpected source of replenishment. I didn't have to plan meals, cook, clean, or attend events. We fixed our breakfast in a shared kitchen that was stocked (blessedly, by someone else) three times a week. After reading and writing in the morning, we wandered down to the laundry building where three-tiered lunch pails with the names of our apartment awaited us. Nalini, a visual artist from Bombay, told us that they are called tiffin boxes in India and that now tiffin wallahs collect them by the hundreds at homes and deliver them by city trains and bicycles to their owners for lunch. Like curious, hungry children, we'd open each lid: salad, a pasta dish, a vegetable.

I read and wrote again in the afternoon, and then at 7:30, we joined the group (and the mosquitoes joined us all) for dinner outside. For the first time, I saw glowworms. Soon, I began to feel a sense of rhythm to my days though it remained a challenge to trust, observe, ponder. Daily, I wrote in my journal, listened to others talk about their work and lives, and I read.

Vern and I took breaks and briefly visited Florence, studied the art of Italian masters, the frescoes of Fra Angelico and Massacio; again, we melted in the heat as we trudged from museum to museum. We looked up in amazement at the green, white, and pink marble exterior of Santa Maria del Fiore. What patience artists and artisans practiced to add beauty to that space.

On a day visit to Assisi—La Citta Mistica, the Mystical City—we saw pilgrims from all over the world visiting the places the patron saint of the environment, Saint Francis (San Francesco), lived and worked, and the churches that commemorate his life. At the hermitage in the Monte Subasio Park, I watched a slender French boy about seven trying to help his grandmother through the narrow arched door openings and down the steps literally shined by the shoes of countless pilgrims. The boy took his grandmother's hand, and she slowly descended the small, shiny red stone steps, saying, *"Oof, oof."* The little sacrifices family members make can yield wonderful stories. I savored the narrow streets, the rock houses decorated with plants and wondered how the illustrator who was beginning work on woodcuts for my children's book on St. Francis would depict the hills.

I've stressed the importance of knowing the self and how writing can be another path in. Self-knowledge is also helpful in developing persistence because we have to learn a pace that works for us. I've always longed to be an early riser, and like the Australian teacher-author Sylvia Ashton-Warner, wake early and write. The reality is that with too much stillness at five a.m., even if I could drag my sleepy self up, I'd drift back to sleep and soon be enjoying what the Italians call *dolce far niente,* sweetly doing nothing. I've learned when to continue entering text at my computer and when to stop and read or file.

What a privilege to write for weeks in a castle and to savor Italy's grand cities, its verdant hills. Gelato too. Vern and I worked hard at the castle, but we enjoyed the gift we'd been given in spite of the oppressive heat. Oh yes, we didn't savor the bat that occasionally flew through our bedroom. Eek!

The time in the castle reminded me how writing rejuvenates me. I meet so many creative teachers, librarians, professors who, like you, also feel rejuvenated by developing their artistic selves. In a world obsessed by perfecting the body, we are exercising the spirit, asking it to leap and stretch and soar.

Are you now more interested in developing your creative talents? What are some obstacles—papers to grade, tasks at home, sleep, friends and family, e-mail, television? The deeper issues challenge us too: fear, doubt, rejections, the discomfort of sitting still waiting for a good idea or, in revision, searching for the right structure or word. The discouragements in a writer or artist's life can be many. Even if you have no interest in being published, you may also experience all kinds of frustration: the amount of time available, the inevitable gap between your vision and creation.

My friend Carmella, who clearly remembers the impact of her teachers' support in encouraging her to become a writer, says she persists, is lured back to the page by the hope that she will write something better, that the new project will be her best. Fierce determination can be required at times to keep appointments with the self or with a manuscript, to create the habit of returning to our work. Rituals, having a set time or a place that reminds us that verbal exploration matters, all help nudge us to the paper or canvas. I can be high with excitement to begin a new piece or to revise what I entered one day and the following day feel sluggish or discouraged. I rely on my willpower to eliminate other options: cleaning the house or taking the day off. I write. Persistence is what allows us to pursue our work, to improve it, to learn from completing a piece and then from setting off in a new direction. The inventiveness we're nurturing helps us also be more imaginative in our responses to the inevitable setbacks in our writing, photography, composing.

I hope that you're becoming more convinced that your creative work is one of the gifts you bring the world. Think of your favorite color. If you have within you one aspect of that color, an irreproducible sliver, and the world never sees it, no one mourns because the loss is unknown, but the loss is still real. Something that could have been was denied by the owner. Plant the seeds of your creativity and listen for your unique songs.

Our symbols: seeds, labyrinth, earth, feather, water, incense. Today, I send the final imaginary gift, a small wreath made of twigs. The twigs are intertwined, as are our seven practices. We can think of one another repeating the round: valuing our creative selves; nurturing solitude; gathering our materials, the aspects of our lives; exploring our talents; revising; sharing; and then persisting in repeating the journey. What are the seeds we wish to sow—in our lives, our writing or painting, our role as educators, as community leaders? How are we preparing and nurturing ourselves?

The circular journey, symbolized by the wreath, includes practices that assist us to create a more inventive garden, a richer poem, dance, or musical composition. We're also revising our view of our work and ourselves, creating a life in which we gradually develop our full complexity.

I love to learn, and as I write you this final set of letters, I've discovered that I continue to write not only because I have stories or ideas to share but also because I learn from writing. That private pleasure helps lure me back to the page, another circle. Much of learning is often relearning what matters but which we quickly forget in the pressures of our days. Gathering my thoughts for you, reading, and doodling—all taught me.

I often review my life goals and make pie charts of the elements I want in my life. This morning, thinking of you and our letter journey together, I created what I'll call a Dynamic Spiral to describe my ideal days. As I enjoyed drawing and labeling the segment swirls, I discovered that though I've managed to write steadily for a number of years and have given health and wellness more attention recently, I haven't really allotted time for nurturing my creative self, for regular time to stroll and mull, enjoy art and gardening books, visit museums (and I live in Santa Fe!), play the untouched piano, listen to music. I haven't shaped some mental playtime. Though I write and speak about the need for vacations and fallow time, I haven't felt I had time for that. That neglected part of me has been shoved out of the way by my lists, schedules, advocacy goals. Thanks to these letters I've written you, I've concluded that creative play might well enhance all the aspects of my ideal life.

This is my final letter about your creative work, your writing or painting or composing. Though this is not good-bye, I feel a certain sadness sending these pages off. I will miss writing to you, dear teacher. Together, let's hold the seeds, labyrinth, sand, feather, water, incense, and wreath. Value and befriend your creative self. Find encouragement in words of William Butler Yeats that in remaking our song, we're remaking ourselves.

Exploration

Are you familiar with mandalas, the word that means circle in Sanskrit and represents wholeness? After reading about the concept, draw a circle and with colored pens or paints or pictures, fill the circle with your inside self, using images and symbols, no words. Make your inside self visible to yourself.

Filling circles makes me think about abundance. I once taught a course on feasts in which we focused on the concept of abundance whether of memories, light, families, pleasures, celebrations, words, obsessions, the sacred. What feasts, such as feasts of light, feasts of music, feasts for the eye, family feasts, and so on, serve as catalysts that assist you to revise and to return to the circular journey? Describe the feast.

Invitation to Write

Change is slow, but it is more likely to occur when we have a plan, a few clear goals. In your journal or in a place you look at often, write a simple creativity plan for the coming year. Your answers can be brief, but be specific. Date your agreement with yourself.

- How can you remind yourself to value your creative talents?
- When and where will you practice solitude?

- How often will you spend time on your writing or sketching per week? What reading goals would assist your work?
- What would you hope to complete in the year ahead?
- What will inspire you to revise your work?
- How might you share what you create?
- What will assist you to persist in the seven practices?

To end on a deeper note, reflect on the following words from Gerard Manley Hopkins' "As Kingfishers Catch Fire":

"What I do is me: for that I came."

The following poem was inspired by a Texas librarian who confided that she'd been a shy university student who found class participation very difficult. Then, a special professor came into this student's life. How delighted I was to learn that the special teacher was my friend Sylvia Vardell.

Ode to Teachers

I remember

the first day,

how I looked down

hoping you wouldn't see

me,

and when I glanced up,

I saw your smile

shining like a soft light

from deep inside you.

"I'm listening," you encouraged us.

"Come on!"

"Join our conversation,

let us hear your neon certainties,

thorny doubts, tangled angers,"

but for weeks, I hid inside.

I read and reread your notes

praising

my writing,

and you whispered,

"We need you

and your stories

and questions

that like a fresh path

will take us to new vistas."

Slowly, your faith grew

into my courage

and for you—

instead of handing you

a note or apple or flowers—

I raised my hand.

I carry your smile

and faith inside like I carry

my dog's face,

my sister's laugh,

creamy melodies,

the softness of sunrise,

steady blessings of stars,

autumn smell of gingerbread,

the security of a sweater on a chilly day.

Dizzy in Your Eyes

Motivate Students to Persevere

Dear Teacher,

Let's Imagine

Let's imagine schools, campuses, and libraries alive with students and educators learning and exploring together.

Let's imagine schools, campuses, libraries, and textbooks that reflect the resplendent plurality of our country, our many voices and stories.

Let's imagine educational institutions and communities that value teachers and librarians as essential community leaders who transform lives.

Let's imagine communities determined to erase illiteracy, to foster a literacy legacy for all.

Let's imagine dedicated educators who persist in creativity practices to explore and share their talents.

Let's imagine creative and committed educators like you, dear teacher, who believe in the inventive potential of all their students and who steadily practice the art of teaching.

As I walked the streets of Berlin a few years ago, I was reminded of the power of a book, a book I hadn't read since I was a teenager. Whether riding on a small boat for a city tour, visiting museums or the zoo, I was haunted by Anne Frank's voice. Then one afternoon, I turned a corner, and there was her picture announcing a nearby exhibit about her, the companion I knew but had never met except on the page. The magic of words.

As you and I know, and as I've mentioned in these letters, cultures, countries, and history are complex. Recently, my friend Barbara told me about coming to Michigan from Germany as a little girl. Though community agencies were supportive to her immigrant family, her elementary school experience was a lonely one. The nuns and students hissed that she was "a Nazi," a sadness she couldn't bear to share with her parents who were so pleased that their daughter was in a U.S. school and learning English.

In middle school, Barbara innocently stayed after class one day to tell her social studies teacher the correct pronunciation of a German word he'd used. He looked down at her and said that he didn't think that knowing German was anything to be proud of.

How many children, families, adults, religions, and languages have been demeaned in this land that's "our land"? I still hear the Columbian psychologist in the Midwest saying, "The professional woman I was is gone here. When I go in to be an advocate for my child who is disabled, all the principal hears is my accent. He can't hear my intelligence."

Yes, such assumptions and judgments are part of human history, but as a nation, we have higher standards than that, "created equal," right? When will such cruelty end? Tired and unappreciated as educators feel sometimes, we are part of the answer. Exciting, isn't it? It's important to think about such painful scenes and learn from them, to value and develop our emotional knowledge and insights, to use them to connect to the students we teach, letting their stories strengthen our determination to be part of our country's progress. Not all of our students will respond to our efforts, but I've stressed reaching out to *all* our students to remind us that certain students can be ignored, undervalued for a host of reasons: physical or learning disabilities, shyness, because they're new to this country or don't speak English. All our young are vulnerable, our underserved young particularly so. There is no neutral way to be an effective advocate for them. Inspiring Brazilian educator Paolo Freire challenges us to respect our students, to remember that together we are both teachers *and* students, that we need to be engaged with our students in reciprocal learning. Literacy and literature help us cross borders and build community.

I smiled hearing María Hinojosa, the host of NPR's *Latino USA*, say that when she came here as a child from Mexico, she longed to be able to say, "supercalifragilisticexpialidocious," to claim English as her own. How do we remember the minds and imagination that can be obscured by language issues? And how do we remember the longing of those wanting to be heard and noticed, to communicate in English? Their inventive abilities and intelligence can surprise us if we value them and convey our faith. We read testimonials to teachers who "changed my life," "gave me books to read," "inspired me to be a teacher like her." The impact of a librarian in the life of university chancellor and author Tomás Rivera was one of the prompts for writing *Tomás and the Library Lady*.

Educators at all levels leave the profession bitter and cynical, feeling undervalued by colleagues, families, students, politicians. When I read the headline "Scandinavians Top Happiness Poll," I smiled. Apparently, modest expectations were a factor. Is it that the disillusioned educators, though joining the profession to make a difference, felt the testing frenzy, pay, and respect issues left them feeling discouraged, voiceless? Teaching creatively and constructively is a significant challenge, and courage is indeed required to remain committed to the higher calling of expanding the horizons of students, some of whom will be underprepared and indifferent. To gloss this challenge would be unfair. Also unfair is diminishing the importance and necessity of inspiring and effective educators busy preparing our next generation.

In 2004, I had the pleasure of hearing Coretta Scott King, who taught us much about dignity and leadership through her life, grace, and courage. Speaking at the University of Cincinnati's graduation, she said, "The best way to spread democracy is to set an irresistible example." Wonderful words. Let's adapt them. The best way to spread bookjoy is to set an irresistible example. The best way to excite students about the zing of writing is to set an irresistible example. Humans are creatures of habit—where and what we eat, how we spend our weekends. To change the behaviors of students of all ages, we need to foster new habits knowing that change isn't easy; it requires purposeful effort. In motivating ourselves to develop our creativity practices, we also prepare to inspire our students to develop theirs.

At a practical level, as we look at grim dropout statistics, in our technological country, we know that without diplomas and degrees, students increase the possibility of never reaching their potential. To persist, students need to believe that they can succeed. My friend Barbara, a museum educator, reminds me that education is like a roundhouse, and we can offer students diverse ways to enter. Some students need your example and guidance to experience their inventive talents and then motivate themselves to improve their work, to find personal satisfaction through their efforts. You're their guide in exploring more complex work.

Students are taught not by robots but by humans shaped by their society. We can choose to reject stereotypes and superficial values, to give students our faith and help them understand that ours is a world of interconnected humans. Unwilling to dismiss some students as disposable, we can motivate them to persist in believing in themselves even when ignored by others around them. Your support will motivate them to persist in developing their talents, their abilities to think critically, to read broadly, and to express themselves articulately. What power you have, dear teacher.

My friend Doug e-mailed me saying, "When teachers access and practice their own creativity, it enables them to be so much more joyful, effective—and real—in helping children learn to do the same. I tell my preservice teachers that creativity is our birthright; it is who we are, and anyone who says, 'I'm just not creative' doesn't know himself or herself." I hope these letters have helped you reassess your inventiveness.

As you revise your vision of yourself to include your creative talents, you'll enjoy designing more imaginative assignments that serve as catalysts because you'll be facing similar challenges or seeking intriguing catalysts. If you try writing about the sound of the color red or about the color of poetry, for example, and your students try too, you're on your way to collaborative, interesting discoveries about words, metaphors, and language. You'll be fostering a community of inventive learners all exploring together and cheering one another on. By now, you know that I'm not talking about glib or hollow cheering or praise. Only by accepting how important you are in the lives of your students, by having a sincere desire to assist them in progressing beyond what they might imagine, by having the knowledge and training to listen, respect, assess, and mentor constructively can you fulfill your full promise. That zing circles and sings. Hear it?

Should zing, zest, energy be marketed as a cure-all for diseases, aches, depression? To help us lose weight or to dissolve wrinkles? To shower us with financial success? No such luck, *but* investing in your inventive self will bring you a deep, quiet, private happiness, I think, and provide you with gifts to share, unique gifts. By helping your students of all ages develop these practices, you'll be helping each to more fully explore and enjoy her or his talents.

In these letters, sharing the practices that keep me writing, I've braided stories about aspects of my personal life, and my writing, speaking, and advocacy life—the joys and frustrations. I believe even more strongly than I did when I started writing you that by developing our creativity, we enrich our life and the lives of those around us, including our students.

I've avoided differentiating between Creativity, with a capital *C* as in genius, and the creativity we all possess. A friend mentioned that playing a musical instrument wasn't creative if it were merely repetitive. Generally, creativity implies the welling up of a new, novel, inventive approach, solution, idea, and obviously, there are levels of ingenuity. It's the commitment that I cherish and believe in—to yourself, your students, and thus to your community—that slowly makes our world a better place.

Just as our own families are diverse (thank heavens), so are our country and world, our many cultures. Research is more and more confirming that diversity is an asset offering organizations—hospitals, corporations, the media, our legal system, educational institutions—knowledge, new perspectives, solutions, strength, and wisdom.

Your inventive leadership is needed by your peers and profession. You can collaborate with your colleagues and support them in revising their self-perception as leaders if that's necessary. Through your "irresistible example," can you nudge your peers to persist in the seven practices, to motivate their students and foster a school or department that values creativity? My friend, Texas library leader Pat Smith, reminds me, "Don't hesitate to offer people the opportunity to participate in community building."

Librarians and teachers can look perplexed when I refer to them as community leaders. Daily, you and your peers are teaching the next generation, investing in the future. Of course, you're leaders, potential leaders, though some relinquish the opportunity to be actively engaged. "There is in you what is beyond you," wrote poet Paul Valery. How's that for optimism?

You and I belong to many communities. To be positive members bringing our unique talents to our tasks, chosen or assigned, we'll need practices that sustain our convictions and enthusiasm. If we become parched, cynical, we cease to be forces, agents for improving the world, our world that can be a gathering of unlived lives. What habits allow you to continue to be or to become a leader with your own style in your professional organizations and at your school, university, or library knowing that "none of us is as smart as all of us," as a Japanese proverb says?

Never doubt the significance of your work. Barbara Jordan spoke of "making America as good as its promise." Like Congresswoman and leader Jordan, dedicated educators don't settle for rhetoric. The old song about each of us letting our little light shine implies valuing, nurturing, and sharing that light for the good of all.

Seed, labyrinth, sand, feather, incense, water, wreath. We value our creativity, the importance of quiet and of gathering our materials, of exploring, developing, and sharing our talents, and the need to persist in our own work, as teachers, advocates, professional and community leaders.

Tip

I think of you when I gaze at the small woven wreath, circle, ring. It is natural, sturdy, intertwined. Like you, I wish to widen the educational circle by welcoming other voices.

Reread your journal and ponder what you've written during our time together. Where do you come from and where do you wish to go—and not just geographically? How can that influence your new phase as a creative person and as a creative teacher?

Exploration for You

Your final aesthetic responses can be concrete or completely abstract. Remember they are for you, reminders of who you are and what you're trying to create as an educator/leader. Sketch, compose a song, or in some inventive way convey the landscapes, cityscapes, or voices that comfort you. Take time to study what you've created and return to this often.

Sketch a companion piece about the kind of learning space you hope to create for your students.

Create a collage of yourself as a unique community leader. The goal is not to focus on the ego but to focus on your community or communities and your role within them.

Invitation to Write

Write a letter to your students. This may be an unsent letter that allows you to articulate the kind of space for exploration you plan to create. Who will feel welcome there? Who will feel challenged but not totally discouraged? How will your students feel about learning, writing, and creative work at the end of the year or semester? Are there new strategies you hope to employ?

What three adjectives would you like students to use to describe you?

Hope

Esperanza

I'm not exactly the same person I was when I began this book, nor are you. We've pondered together and reminded ourselves of the significance of our work as educators and also of the value of being writers and artists ourselves. I strive to make these seven practices a rhythmic part of my life. The practice of solitude, of a mini-retreat, a ritual that refreshes us, invites us to reflect on our role within our various communities: geographic, ethnic, professional. To thrive, for the full blossoming of the self in all its complexity, we need quiet to nurture resilience, and we need engagement with our colleagues, creating relationships that support the full potential of our diverse students.

I smile remembering how furious my young son became every July at "Back to School" signs proclaiming sales and bargains. He wanted the summer, those lazy, carefree days, to stretch on endlessly. Isn't that what we all want when we're happy, to grasp the clock's hands firmly? I feel that way about ending my letters to you. As happens when I'm deep in a book, I've noticed and savored and pondered with more enthusiasm because I knew I could share all kinds of topics with you because educators are curious.

I love the words of chef Julia Child, "It's a shame to be caught up in something that doesn't absolutely make you tremble with joy." Do you feel that way some days? I'm fortunate to know amazing teachers—like you. I think far more teachers and librarians might feel this pleasure were they to release their full talents, talents we need, their students need, talents that would warm the educators' own lives.

Let's remain incurably hopeful. Together, let's surprise ourselves by the depth and creativity of our commitment to our students.

Joy, dear teacher! Joy!

Pat

Questions for Exploration

We hope you enjoy exploring the following questions either for personal reflection or with your book club, preservice classes, alternative certification classes, homeschool teachers, inservice sessions, school read programs, your community of family and friends, or with your professional learning community.

1. A quote by Cervantes reinforced Pat Mora's determination to spend time writing. Have you been moved by any experiences or notable quotes (possibly from this book) to write or explore some other creative facet of yourself? If so, when and where? How has that moment been significant in your day-to-day life?

2. Which of the seven creative practices resonates with you the most? Which one has (or will) have the largest impact of your personal or professional practices?

3. In what way has your personal definition of creativity been broadened after reading *Zing!?* How can you and your colleagues use your new collective definition to empower yourselves, one another, and your students?

4. Time is a thread throughout this book—as a necessity for growth but also as precious and fleeting. Has this book changed your concept of time? Have you rearranged your time and/or reordered your priorities to make room to employ the seven creative practices professionally? Personally?

5. How has this book helped you to uncover and develop your imaginative self? Did you discover any new strengths or identify any areas that need improvement?

6. Discuss/share which of the many exploration prompts led you to a new revelation about yourself or your work with students. How has this realization impacted your thinking or actions?

7. Although educators may never learn or understand every language or culture they encounter in their classrooms or school, what effect can attitude have on how you choose to welcome and interact with diverse students and their families?

8. Mora asserts that educators must nurture their students' courage. What does this mean to you and what are some ways you plan to further your efforts and intentions in this respect to produce brave and self-confident students?

9. Throughout the book, Mora first addresses how teachers and librarians can implement the practices in their lives and, in turn, how educators can help their students with the practice. What do you think of this structure? What is being implied by this parallelism, and how does it affect your idea of the teacher-student relationship?

10. The creative journey can be a solitary one whether one is a parent, educator, administrator, or beginning artist. What have you learned from this book that can sustain you on your journey?

Suggested Reading

I've read, reveled in, and learned from the following books through the years. Many of these authors have written other books I also value.

Atchity, Kenneth. *A Writer's Time: A Guide to the Creative Process, From Vision Through Revision*

Atwood, Margaret. *Negotiating with the Dead: A Writer on Writing*

Brande, Dorothea. *Becoming a Writer*

Cameron, Julia. *The Artist's Way: A Spiritual Path to Higher Creativity*

Csikszentmihali, Mihaly. *Finding Flow: The Psychology of Engagement with Everyday Life*

Dillard, Annie. *The Writing Life*

Drury, John. *The Poetry Dictionary*

Goldberg, Natalie. *Writing Down the Bones*

Kunitz, Stanley. *The Wild Braid: A Poet Reflects on a Century in the Garden (with Genine Lentine)*

Lamott, Anne. *Bird by Bird*

Lindberg, Anne Morrow. *Gift from the Sea*

Malone, Nancy M. *Walking a Literary Labyrinth: A Spirituality of Reading*

Neruda, Pablo. *Memoirs*

Oliver, Mary. *A Poetry Handbook: A Prose Guide to Understanding and Writing Poetry*

Rilke, Rainer Maria. *Letters to a Young Poet*

Ueland, Brenda. *If You Want to Write: A Book about Art, Independence and Spirit* [Caveat: This book published in 1938 contains some cultural attitudes that make me groan; that aside, it is a helpful book.]

Welty, Eudora. *One Writer's Beginnings*

Other Books by Pat Mora

NONFICTION

House of Houses

Nepantla: Essays from the Land in the Middle

POETRY

Adobe Odes

Aunt Carmen's Book of Practical Saints

Agua Santa: Holy Water

Communion

Borders

Chants

YOUNG ADULT

Dizzy in Your Eyes: Poems About Love

My Own True Name: New and Selected Poems for Young Adults

CHILDREN'S BOOKS

Gracias, Thanks

A Piñata in a Pine Tree: A Latino Twelve Days of Christmas

Wiggling Pockets Los bolsillos saltarines

Book Fiesta: Celebrate Children's Day/Book Day, Celebremos El día de los niños/El día de los libros

Abuelos

Here, Kitty, Kitty!/¡Ven, gatita, ven!

Sweet Dreams/Dulces sueños

Join Hands

Let's Eat! ¡A comer!

Yum! ¡MmMm! ¡Qué Rico!

¡Marimba! Animales A to Z

Doña Flor: A Tall Tale About a Giant Woman with a Great, Big Heart

The Song of Francis and the Animals

A Library for Juana: The World of Sor Juana Inés

Maria Paints the Hills

The Bakery Lady: La señora de la panadería

Love to Mamá: A Tribute to Mothers (editor)

The Race of Toad and Deer

The Night the Moon Fell

The Rainbow Tulip

This Big Sky

Delicious Hullabaloo: Pachanga deliciosa

Tomás and the Library Lady

Confetti: Poems for Children

Uno, Dos, Tres: One, Two, Three

The Gift of the Poinsettia: El regalo de la flor de nochebuena (with Charles Ramírez Berg)

Agua, Agua, Agua

Pablo's Tree

The Desert Is My Mother: El desierto es mi madre

Listen to the Desert: Oye al desierto

A Birthday Basket for Tía

CORWIN

A SAGE Company

The Corwin logo—a raven striding across an open book—represents the union of courage and learning. Corwin is committed to improving education for all learners by publishing books and other professional development resources for those serving the field of PreK–12 education. By providing practical, hands-on materials, Corwin continues to carry out the promise of its motto: **"Helping Educators Do Their Work Better."**